The Illustrated Encyclopaedia of Dangerous Animals

Sami Bayly

A Lothian Children's Book

Published in Australia and New Zealand in 2020
by Hachette Australia
Level 17, 207 Kent Street, Sydney NSW 2000
www.hachettechildrens.com.au

Copyright © Samantha Bayly 2020

This book is copyright. Apart from any fair dealing for the purposes of private study,
research, criticism or review permitted under the *Copyright Act 1968*, no part may
be stored or reproduced by any process without prior written permission. Enquiries
should be made to the publisher.

 A catalogue record for this book is available from the National Library of Australia

ISBN 978 0 7344 2001 5 (hardback)

Cover design, internal design and typesetting by Astred Hicks, Design Cherry
Colour reproduction by Splitting Image
Printed by 1010 Printing, China

Contents

Introduction
7

African Buffalo
9

African Giant Swallowtail
10

Africanised Honey Bee
13

Alligator Snapping Turtle
14

Asian Giant Hornet
17

Australian Magpie
18

Bibron's Stiletto Snake
21

Black Marlin
22

Blacklegged Tick
25

Blue Dragon
26

Blue-and-yellow Macaw
29

Boomslang
30

Brazilian Wandering Spider
33

Bulldog Ant
34

Cane Toad
37

Carnivorous Caterpillar
38

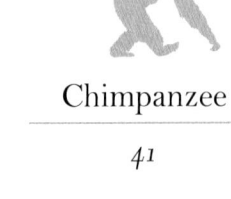
Chimpanzee
41

Coffin Ray
42

Common Hippopotamus
45

Crown-of-thorns Starfish
46

Deer Mouse
49

Electric Eel
50

Flamboyant Cuttlefish
53

Geography Cone Snail
54

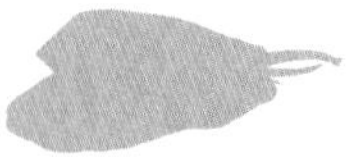

German Cockroach
57

Giant Otter
58

Gila Monster
61

Golden Poison Frog
62

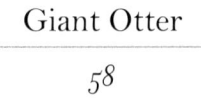
Goliath Tigerfish
65

Greater Slow Loris
66

Greater Weever Fish
69

Hooded Pitohui
70

Human Botfly
73

Indian Red Scorpion
74

Irukandji Jellyfish
77

Kissing Bug
78

Komodo Dragon
81

Leopard Seal
82

Moose
85

Mosaic Crab
86

Oriental Rat Flea
89

Ostrich
90

Pork Tapeworm
93

Red-bellied Piranha
94

Red-headed Mouse Spider
97

Red Devil Squid
98

Red Kangaroo
101

Red Lionfish
102

Reef Stonefish
105

Rough-skinned Newt
106

Shortfin Mako Shark
109

Six-spot Burnet Moth
110

Southern Blue-ringed Octopus
113

Spider-tailed Horned Viper
114

Tasmanian Devil
117

Tiger Pufferfish
118

Titan Triggerfish
121

Vampire Bat
122

Wolverine
125

Yellow Fever Mosquito
126

About the author
128

Introduction

This is not your average dangerous animals book! By the end of it, I hope you've learnt some mind-blowing facts about animals that you probably didn't even know were deadly, and that you appreciate them for their unique contributions to the natural environment.

It is my mission to shine a light on the more misunderstood species in the animal kingdom. In this book, I wanted to explore the traits that make these creatures unique and look at the function behind their dangerous adaptations – why have they evolved to protect themselves in the ways they do? The answers are truly fascinating.

As with the animals in my first book, *The Illustrated Encyclopaedia of Ugly Animals*, dangerous animals quite often have misconceptions surrounding them. Because dangerous animals are a nuisance or pose a threat to humans, they are too often seen as something to fear or kill instead of the fascinating creatures they are.

Every one of these sixty animals is a brilliant combination of strange and dangerous, and I loved painting them and their quirky attributes in watercolour. I hope I have showcased their true magnificence.

Sami Bayly

Syncerus caffer

African Buffalo

Syncerus caffer
(sin-seer-us caf-er)

Description

African buffalo are enormous, growing up to 1.5 metres tall and weighing up to 800 kilograms. African buffalo grow thicker skin around their neck, in order to protect them from predators and other buffalo. They share an interesting relationship with a bird called the oxpecker. The oxpecker sits on buffalos' backs and feeds on ticks, lice and fleas that can be found crawling there.

Danger Factor

Despite their size, African buffalo can run as fast as 59 kilometres per hour, so it is no wonder that these easily aggravated mammals can cause a lot of harm to those in their path. In fact, these buffalo kill more hunters than any other animal in their region. Instead of running away when injured or threatened, African buffalo charge directly at the threat, using their large horns to toss the victim into the air. In Africa they are one of the 'big five' – alongside the lion, rhinoceros, elephant and leopard. The big five is a list of animals that pose the most danger to hunters.

Conservation Status

LEAST CONCERN

The African buffalo is preyed upon by lions and sometimes has altercations with African elephants. It is also a favourite of trophy and meat hunters. These animals were threatened by an infectious disease called rinderpest, which massively reduced their population during the 1800s. Fortunately, their range remains extensive.

Diet

Quite often the largest and most dangerous animals are herbivores and do not actually eat or prey on other animals. Instead, they use their size and strength to protect them from predators. This is the case for the African buffalo.

This species eats predominantly leaves and grasses, feeding mostly at night. During the day, they chew cud in order to extract as much energy and nutrients from their food as possible. Cud is a portion of food that ruminants like buffalo and cows bring up from their stomachs and back into their mouths.

Location/Habitat

African buffalo are robust animals and can live anywhere with a water source and consistent supply of grass and leaves. Typically, they are found in lowland rainforests, grasslands and woodlands within the sub-Saharan region of Africa. There is safety in numbers and so these animals often live in herds of a few hundred, sometimes even up to a thousand. This can be dangerous for any animals that find themselves in the way of a stampede.

Fun Facts

→ African buffalo have good memories and have been known to injure people who have hurt them in the past.
→ If a baby buffalo loses its mother, another adult buffalo will often accompany it and care for it until they can be reunited.
→ African buffalo have smooth tongues, unlike cows whose tongues can be compared to sandpaper.

African Giant Swallowtail

Papilio antimachus
(pap-ill-e-o anti-mak-us)

Description

The African giant swallowtail is the largest butterfly in Africa and one of the largest in the world, so it is no surprise that these insects are often compared to birds when flying. After all, they have a wingspan of up to 23 centimetres!

Danger Factor

As well as being large, these butterflies are also very poisonous. During their caterpillar stage, they eat leaves full of toxins called glycosides. These toxins become even more dangerous as they are digested and the butterfly that emerges from the cocoon is deadly to anything that consumes it.

Conservation Status

DATA DEFICIENT

There are so few African giant swallowtails seen in the wild that there is not enough data to know what their conservation status is. However, scientists are almost certain they are extremely rare and in desperate need of our help.

The only threats these insects face are human ones. Other animals, such as birds, have learnt how deadly they are and know to steer clear of them. Humans pose a threat through habitat destruction and by poaching the butterflies for their magnificent wings.

Diet

During their butterfly stage, African giant swallowtails eat flower nectar. It is thought that during their caterpillar stage they feed on the leaves of the climbing oleander (*Strophanthus gratus*), a species of plant that has attractive and fragrant white, pink and purple flowers. It is this seemingly innocent plant that stays in their system until adulthood and makes them so toxic.

Location/Habitat

African giant swallowtails are found in the rainforests of west and central Africa and can be very difficult to spot. Males can be seen closer to the ground, usually near water, but females spend all of their time high in the tree canopy. They are even more elusive as caterpillars, and it is still unclear what they actually look like at that stage.

Fun Facts

- African giant swallowtails possess another defence mechanism: they can emit a cloud of stinky chemicals when disturbed.
- The first recorded European sighting of an African giant swallowtail was in 1782.
- It is thought the toxins in a climbing oleander are so strong they could even kill a hippopotamus (found on page 45).

Papilio antimachus

Apis mellifera scutellata Lepeletier

Africanised Honey Bee

Apis mellifera scutellata Lepeletier
(ay-pis mely-fear-a skew-tell-a-ta lep-el-et-ee-er)

Description

Africanised honey bees and European honey bees are almost identical. They both feature a pair of wings, 6 legs and a hairy back, known as a thorax. The main difference is that the Africanised honey bee is slightly darker in colour, smaller and behaves more aggressively.

Danger Factor

Also known as killer bees, these insects are just 1–2 centimetres long but can really pack a punch. In fact, it is estimated they have caused the deaths of approximately 1000 people who were allergic since their introduction to Brazil, where they are commonly found. Africanised honey bees will defend their nest from any threats and have been known to swarm and chase trespassers up to 1.5 kilometres, delivering hundreds of stings. While they do not contain more or stronger venom than other honey bees, they pose more of a threat because of their aggressive behaviour. But to label them 'killer bees' is not fair – after all, they are simply defending their hive (and doing a very thorough job of it).

Conservation Status

NOT EVALUATED

In the 1950s, some African honey bees were imported to Brazil to help increase honey production. Unfortunately, a number of swarms escaped and mated with the local European honey bee population. This new poly-hybrid was named the Africanised honey bee and is now considered an invasive species. It is likely this species will continue to spread as they are good at adapting to their environment.

Diet

These bees feed on nectar and pollen, which they transform into honey. They are incredible pollinators and because of this they are valuable members of their environment and also very useful to humans. Honey bees pollinate many crops and are vital to the agriculture industry.

Location/Habitat

Africanised honey bees have slowly populated many parts of South America and all of Central America. They are even making their way up to parts of North America. These bees nest in a range of places, including wood piles, tree hollows, logs and urban structures like chimneys and roofs.

Fun Facts

- It would take around 1000 bee stings to kill an adult without a bee allergy.
- Queen bees can live for up to 3 years, whereas worker bees live for only 1.5 months.
- It is said that if running away from a swarm of bees, you should not enter water to escape, as they will wait for you to surface.
- A queen bee is created by her being fed royal jelly in the larvae stage. Royal jelly is a white jelly-like mixture of mandibular and hypopharyngeal gland secretions.

Alligator Snapping Turtle

Macrochelys temminckii

(macro-chel-ees tem-in-key-eye)

Description

This is not a turtle you would want to mess with! The alligator snapping turtle is both enormous and very heavy. Males range from 60–100 centimetres long and weigh an average of 75 kilograms. The females are only slightly smaller.

Danger Factor

Have you been wondering why this turtle is called alligator snapping turtle? Or why it is featured in this book of dangerous animals? Well, its common name comes from the ridges that run down its back and from its mighty sharp jaws which snap shut on nearby prey or those who pose a threat. Using a bite force measuring device, these turtles have been documented to inflict approximately 450 kilograms of force when they chomp down. That is enough to go through bone! However, fortunately for us, they very rarely attack humans unless provoked, due to their slow and docile personalities.

Conservation Status

VULNERABLE

This powerful species of turtle is unfortunately considered vulnerable because their habitats are being cleared and they are hunted for their meat and shells. The alligator snapping turtle plays an important role in the environment by eating decomposing animals and plants. Maintaining and improving their population size is essential to this species' survival, and for the quality of their ecosystem.

Diet

This carnivorous creature has a lure-like tongue that sits within its mouth. Pink in colour, it wiggles about like a small worm and attracts fish, frogs and molluscs. However, the turtles also use their camouflage and slow-moving actions to prey on small birds, mammals and even other turtles! They can snap smaller prey clean in half or swallow them whole.

Location/Habitat

Alligator snapping turtles can hold their breath underwater for up to 50 minutes and prefer to spend their days in lakes, rivers or other bodies of water in the south-eastern United States. Generally preferring being hidden by overhanging foliage and fallen logs and rocks, the females only surface occasionally to lay eggs, which makes these reptiles difficult to spot.

Fun Facts

- The collective name for these animals is a 'dole' or 'bale'.
- There is an alligator snapping turtle living at the Australian Reptile Park in Sydney, Australia. This turtle was found in a Sydney drain and was most likely illegally imported as a pet. He is named Leonardo.
- These turtles are the largest freshwater turtle in North America.
- Alligator snapping turtles are not able to retract their bulky heads back into their shells.
- While they can live up to 70 years, they generally only make it to approximately 25.

Macrochelys temminckii

Vespa mandarinia

Asian Giant Hornet

Vespa mandarinia
(ves-pa man-dar-in-e-a)

Description

These sizable hornets have an 8-centimetre wingspan and can reach 5 centimetres long, not including an additional 6-millimetre stinger found on their tail end. It is this stinger that makes the Asian giant hornet so dangerous.

Danger Factor

The Asian giant hornet's sting has venom that is known to cause 30–50 deaths a year in Japan, where they are commonly found. The different chemicals in the venom can cause breathing issues, worsening pain and tissue deterioration, and can even attract other hornets. Many fatalities are due to allergic reactions to toxins in the venom.

Conservation Status

NOT EVALUATED

Many people consider the Asian giant hornet a nuisance. This is due to their reputation for attacking bee hives and other wasps in groups. They will often bite their victims to death and bring the bodies back to feed their young. This mass slaughter of other species has an impact on insect populations and the ecosystems of the region.

Diet

In its adult stage, these hornets mainly eat insects such as beetles, bees and other wasps. They have also been known to feed on hornworms, tree sap and fruit.

Location/Habitat

Commonly found in Japan, the Asian giant hornet lives around the south-eastern and eastern areas of Asia, as their name suggests. They dig nests up to 60 centimetres deep in forest or mountainous areas, and sometimes even use the pre-existing dig sites of mice and rats.

Fun Facts

- Young hornets feed on meals regurgitated for them by adult hornets. These are typically a mixture of bees and other small insects and are full of nutrients.
- It is suspected that Asian giant hornets only live for around 3–5 months.
- Unlike many bees, the stinger of the Asian giant hornet does not last just one sting. It can be used over and over again.
- There is a species of bee, the Japanese honey bee, which has evolved to counter the attacks of the Asian giant hornet. They will swarm a single hornet and beat their wings fast, creating a lethal level of carbon dioxide around the hornet in order to kill it.
- The Asian giant hornet is thought to be the largest wasp in the world.

Australian Magpie

Gymnorhina tibicen
(gym-nor-ina tib-i-sen)

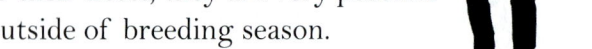

Description

Australian magpies average 40 centimetres in length and weigh just 300 grams. Despite their regular habit of swooping those who walk too close to their nests, they are very peaceful birds outside of breeding season.

Danger Factor

When it comes to breeding season, male Australian magpies implement impressive defensive parenting strategies in order to protect their young, such as swooping, squawking, clawing and pecking. There have been multiple occasions in the recent past in which humans have been injured by these birds, including severe eye and face wounds, and one incident even led to a death. But not all male magpies are this aggressive. Most situations end with a simple scare, so to reduce your chances of being swooped this breeding season follow these simple steps: be alert to their unique song (they are said to sound like a flute), wear sunglasses and a hat, and keep an eye on the birds, since they often attack when their victim's back is turned.

Conservation Status

LEAST CONCERN

The Australian magpie has a large population size, which is predicted to increase.

Because these birds are native to Australia, there are measures in place to prevent them from being killed by humans, or having their eggs taken.

Animals that prey on the magpie include foxes, cats and dogs, so it is important to make sure your pets are kept within their yards at all times, unless on a leash.

Diet

Like many other species of native Australian bird, the magpie feeds on critters like insects, spiders, worms and snails, and will occasionally feast on slightly larger animals, such as lizards and frogs. They typically search on the ground for these foods.

Location/Habitat

Like their name suggests, the Australian magpie can be found throughout Australia, and also in parts of southern New Guinea.

Whether it be a park, dense bushland with nearby open spaces, or a cityscape with a few trees, the magpie will make itself at home. Its ability to nest just about anywhere is the reason so many are affected by its defensive parenting.

Fun Facts

- Australian magpies are nicknamed 'flute birds' because of their magnificent call.
- They have been known to have great memories, often recalling those who treated them well and those who did not.
- You will often see magpies laying in the dirt with their wings outstretched. They are not injured or sick, but rather, they are sunning themselves in order to remove unwanted parasites.
- Their nests can be comprised of grass, sticks, twigs, wool and even animal or human hair!

Gymnorhina tibicen

Atractaspis bibronii

Bibron's Stiletto Snake

Atractaspis bibronii
(a-track-ta-spis bib-roni-eye)

Description

Reaching approximately 30–40 centimetres on average, Bibron's stiletto snakes have been documented to grow as long as 80 centimetres.

After the Mozambique spitting cobra and puff adder, the stiletto snake causes the third highest number of serious snake bites in South Africa. This is because of their likeness to a large worm and non-toxic snake species, which makes them appear non-threatening to those who decide to handle them.

Danger Factor

These snakes have long, thin and hollow fangs that inject a cytotoxic (causes damage to cells) venom into their victims, both animals and humans. Although not usually fatal to humans, this toxin causes severe pain, swelling, tissue damage and in some cases, loss of fingers. The best way to avoid this fate is to not handle snakes unless you are a trained professional.

Conservation Status

NOT EVALUATED

The conservation status of Bibron's stiletto snake is not entirely known. These snakes are a burrowing species and so it is rare to come across them in the wild, but those who do are encouraged to leave them alone. Further, they are sometimes misidentified for other snake species.

Fortunately, it is thought they face very few threats and are of little value within the pet trade.

Diet

Stiletto snakes remain underground while hunting and feeding, feasting on a range of lizards, frogs, rodents and even other snakes. They use their sharp fangs and flexible heads to inject venom into their prey.

Location/Habitat

They spend most of their lives under the soil throughout much of South Africa, Namibia, Eswatini and Botswana. They have been known to emerge from the soil in the early evening when it is warm, or after heavy rain.

Fun Facts

- These snakes were previously known as 'mole adders', since they were often mistaken for mole snakes.
- Their name, 'stiletto snake', was given to them because their long, thin fangs resemble stiletto daggers. These were knives created in the 15th century and were predominantly used by assassins.

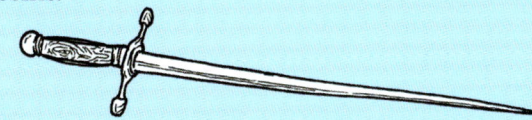

- They have a short, spiked tail which they often use to prick anyone or anything holding onto them.
- A unique ability that stiletto snakes have evolved is to have their fangs sit on the exterior of their mouths, so that even when closed they have the ability to bite. This makes them extra dangerous to handle.
- There is no antivenom for these snakes. The only treatment is to reduce pain and wait.

Black Marlin

Istiompax indica
(eye-sti-om-pax in-di-ka)

Description

Able to grow to a whopping 4.5 metres long and weighing up to 700 kilograms, the black marlin is a monstrous fish. Over millions of years, this fish has evolved incredible features to help it hunt and survive. These features, along with its ability to swim incredibly fast, make it a perfectly dangerous underwater machine.

Danger Factor

Black marlin are considered apex predators, meaning they have no natural predators and are at the top of the food chain. Black marlin have a long, sword-like structure on their face, known as a 'bill', and have been known to impale fishers after being captured and pulled onto boats. On rare occasions, they've even impaled divers while swimming.

Conservation Status

DATA DEFICIENT

The black marlin is caught through both commercial and recreational fishing and is often captured as bycatch by long-lines. After being caught, they are often eaten as sashimi. Unfortunately, there is not enough information available to know the full range and population of this species, resulting in its data deficient conservation status.

Diet

This marlin feeds on a variety of sea creatures, and has been documented eating squid, octopus, fish, cephalopods and crustaceans. They use their incredible bills to stab and cut their prey before consuming it, an intense method that is very impressive to see.

Location/Habitat

You might think that, because of their hefty size, these fish are found in wide-open areas. In fact, they live close to reefs and land masses. Most often found at depths of approximately 100 metres, the black marlin lives throughout the tropical and subtropical Indo-Pacific, including the coasts of Australia.

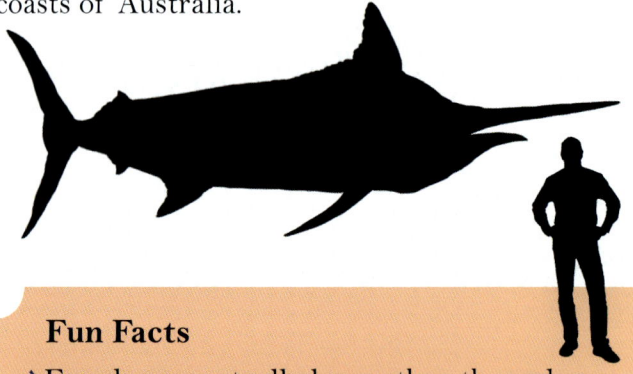

Fun Facts

- Females are actually larger than the males, making this species sexually dimorphic.
- They can live for 9–12 years on average.
- It is thought that this fish can swim as fast as a cheetah can run!
- A massive black marlin was captured off the coast of Queensland, Australia, in 2018, weighing in at almost 650 kilograms. It was thought to be 15 years old. Unfortunately, it died while being reeled in.

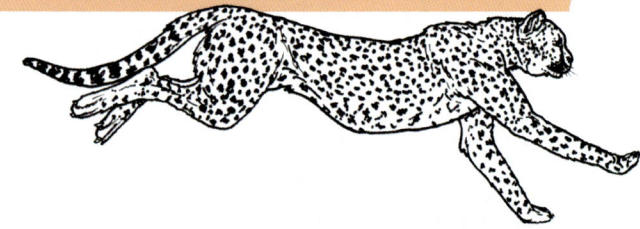

Istiompax indica

Ixodes scapularis

Blacklegged Tick

Ixodes scapularis
(ix-o-dees scap-you-lar-is)

Description

2-4 millimetres

For such small creatures (they are only the size of a sesame seed), the blacklegged tick can cause an incredible amount of pain and suffering. They are often difficult to spot and like to live in areas of the body such as the armpit, groin and scalp.

Ticks are members of the arachnid family, meaning they are related to the Brazilian wandering spider (33), the red-headed mouse spider (97) and the Indian red scorpion (74).

Danger Factor

The blacklegged tick is renowned for being the transmitter of Lyme disease. Symptoms include a bullseye rash around the bite, fatigue, arthritis, severe headaches, heart palpitations, facial paralysis and neurological disorders. If these ticks are not removed within 36–48 hours of biting into a person, the person's risk of being infected with Lyme disease significantly increases. In the case of other animals, these ticks can cause paralysis, and infestations of them can even result in death.

Conservation Status

NOT EVALUATED

It may seem as though the blacklegged tick is of no significance to the animal kingdom, however they are an incredibly valuable food source to a variety of creatures, including guinea hens and opossums, and they also help control the population of many other species. They can take down small rodents all the way to sick deer and even moose. Although this may be seen as a negative, it is important to keep in mind that all creatures, no matter how annoying, have evolved to serve a purpose within their ecosystem. Whether it is a lion taking down an antelope or a group of ticks, both are involved in the natural processes of life.

Diet

During their relatively short lives, the blacklegged tick will only consume 3 blood meals from their hosts. These meals occur in correlation to significant physical changes in the tick's life: moulting from larva to nymph, and from nymph to adult, in order for an adult to lay eggs. They feed to provide themselves with enough energy to complete these vital tasks.

Location/Habitat

These ticks live within the north-eastern, north-central and mid-Atlantic regions of the United States. They reside wherever they can find their favourite hosts. These hosts include deer, rodents, dogs and humans. However, blacklegged ticks are most commonly found in deciduous forest habitats.

FUN FACTS

- Blacklegged ticks live as long as 2 years.
- These ticks are also known as 'deer ticks'.
- In a single egg-laying period, females will lay from 1500–2000 eggs.
- Your chances of catching Lyme disease depends on 3 factors: what species the tick is, where it was before it bit you, and how long it was feeding on you.

Blue Dragon

Glaucus atlanticus
(glaw-kuss at-lan-tee-kuss)

Description

The blue dragon is a small species of sea slug, which reaches lengths of just 3 centimetres. The blue dragon also goes by the more formal term, nudibranch.

When you see them, you are most likely seeing them floating upside down, with their colourful belly facing upwards, which they keep on show to help them blend in with the water below them. Their other side is silver and helps them blend in with the sea surface when seen from underneath. This fantastic adaptation is known as 'countershading' and helps them stay concealed from predators both above and below.

Danger Factor

Blue dragons are able to eat certain poisonous creatures and store their victims' nematocysts (small stinging cells) in the tips of their own wing-like extremities to then use against any predators. These stings not only inflict other sea creatures, but also humans. After many such meals, a blue dragon builds up toxin stores in their own body and can unleash a mighty sting. Stings to humans can be incredibly painful, causing welts, swelling, increased heart rate and vomiting. For the young, elderly or allergic, there is a risk of death.

Conservation Status

NOT EVALUATED

Due to the vast area of ocean that the blue dragon resides in, as well as their tiny size, it is quite tricky to know the range and population of this species.

You might have seen these small ocean dwellers washed up on the beach. This is because their movements are controlled by the weather and they are often thrown about. Even so, it is thought that their numbers are high.

Diet

Despite their small size and slow movements, the blue dragon is actually a scavenging predator. They feed on blue bottles (also known as Portuguese man o' war).

Location/Habitat

Blue dragons can be found throughout open, warm and tropical waters, including the Pacific, Indian and Atlantic oceans.

Fun Facts

- The blue dragon has an air bubble in its stomach which keeps it afloat, letting it drift between the sea levels.
- A group of these nudibranches is called a 'blue fleet'.
- They are hermaphrodites, meaning an individual can produce both sperm and eggs. However, they still need another blue dragon to fertilise the eggs.

Glaucus atlanticus

Ara ararauna

Blue-and-yellow Macaw

Ara ararauna
(air-a air-a-rown-a)

Description

In this case, it is not the individual bird (the blue-and-yellow macaw) that is dangerous on its own, but rather the bacteria, *Chlamydia psittaci*, which is present on it. The bacteria pictured is invisible to the naked eye and can only be uncovered through a microscope.

Danger Factor

This dangerous bacteria can be transmitted to humans, where it turns into the infectious disease, psittacosis. Commonly referred to as 'parrot fever', it is transmitted from birds to humans through the birds' droppings which, when dry, turn into dust-like particles and can be inhaled by humans. The effects of psittacosis vary from a mild illness to more severe symptoms like pneumonia, hepatitis and inflammation of the heart or brain. If not treated properly, it may cause death.

One of those species highly impacted because of its common pet status and caged environment is the blue-and-yellow macaw. In order to avoid catching this disease, use precautions when cleaning cages or handling birds.

Conservation Status

NOT EVALUATED

Since the bacteria responsible for causing harm is not an animal or plant, it cannot be given a conservation status. However, it is not considered useful or beneficial to either humans or animals and there are efforts in place to limit its spread.

Diet

Since it is bacteria and technically a living organism, *Chlamydia psittaci* needs to eat in order to have the energy required to reproduce. It absorbs nutrients from its host.

Location/Habitat

The bacteria is not picky when it comes to which type of bird it lives on and affected species include parrots, chickens, cockatiels, ducks, turkeys and more. However, it is frequently documented among macaws because they are such common pets and live in cages which house the bacteria.

Fun Facts

- In rare cases, you can become infected by a bird biting you or if you are in close contact to its mouth.
- The people most at risk are vets, pet shop workers, zookeepers, bird owners and those who work in the poultry industry.
- To know whether a bird is infected, look out for inflamed eyes, low appetite, diarrhoea and trouble breathing. It is important to know that not all infected birds show symptoms.
- Catching psittacosis will not stop you catching it again. You can contract the disease as many times as you are exposed to it.

Boomslang

Dispholidus typus
(dis-foe-lee-dus tie-pus)

Description

Reaching a whopping 1.5 metres in length, these snakes are swift and slender. They dart through branches, remaining hidden in order to hunt, while using their large eyes to help them see better than any other species of snake.

They are sexually dimorphic, and females and males are quite different colours. In this species, the males are much more vibrant and can be shades of green and yellow. The females are more often a greenish brown colour.

Danger Factor

Like many snakes, the boomslang is venomous. Their venom is unusual, however, in that it is hemotoxic and prevents normal blood clotting. This means that victims will continue to bleed internally and externally after being bitten. If left untreated, a boomslang bite can be fatal. However, it is not common to be bitten by a boomslang because they avoid humans and other animals.

Conservation Status

NOT EVALUATED

Very little is known about the threats and predators that the boomslang faces. However, due to its well-camouflaged body and fast-moving action, it is thought these snakes are successful in avoiding predators that come their way. Unfortunately, they cannot avoid everything, and they are known to be preyed upon by larger birds as well as other boomslangs.

Diet

Using its fast moving, well-hidden body, the boomslang will hide in trees and strike out when its prey approaches, rarely leaving without a meal. They eat eggs, birds, lizards, frogs and snakes.

Location/Habitat

The boomslang is indigenous to Africa, and is widely distributed throughout the continent, including southern and central areas such as Zimbabwe, Botswana and Namibia.

They are arboreal reptiles and live in short trees and shrubs which help them stay camouflaged. Occasionally they will venture to the ground to sunbake or hunt.

Fun Facts

- Boomslangs can open their mouths up to 170 degrees!
- Their name, 'boomslang', is Afrikaans for 'tree snake'.
- They have been known to eat chameleons.
- The boomslang is one of a few snake species that is solenoglyphous, which means it can fold its fangs back into the roof of its mouths after using them. This position makes it look almost as though the snake is chewing down on its victim when releasing the venom.

Dispholidus typus

Phoneutria nigriventer

Brazilian Wandering Spider

Phoneutria nigriventer
(phone-a-tree-a nig-riv-en-ter)

Description

There are actually eight different species under the genus of *Phoneutria*, but it is the Brazilian wandering spider that is covered in many small brown hairs and measures around 15 centimetres across. These spiders certainly look dangerous!

Danger Factor

Not only do they look frightening, but the Brazilian wandering spider is one of the most venomous spiders in the world, with a record of killing humans. Symptoms of their bite include nausea and blurred vision. Despite their potential to be deadly to humans, their bites are not usually lethal. This is because when the spider bites the predator or prey, it does not inject all of its toxic venom. Instead, it uses just a small amount which will immobilise and stop the threat. This clever survival strategy ensures that the spider saves the left-over venom to protect itself while waiting to replenish its supplies. Antivenom has only been needed in 2.3% of cases.

Conservation Status

NOT EVALUATED

The conservation status of these spiders is unknown.

They can be kept as pets, but in order to do so you must hold a Dangerous Wild Animals licence in some countries.

Diet

The name 'wandering spiders' is given to them because they do not build webs. Instead, they wander around the forest floor throughout the night and hide beneath logs during the day.

They mostly hunt other spiders and insects but have also been known to hunt and eat small reptiles, mice and frogs.

Location/Habitat

Like their name suggests, the Brazilian wandering spider is found in Brazil. They sometimes accidentally travel to Europe and North America in banana shipments.

Fun Facts

- They are also known as 'banana spiders' because they like to hide among the fruit.
- The Brazilian wandering spider lives for just 1–2 years.
- Their upstretched front legs are a defensive action to ward off predators. They only bite or attack if they are aggravated or scared.
- Their scientific name, *Phoneutria*, translates to 'murderess' in Greek.
- Females often attack males after mating.

Bulldog Ant

Myrmecia pyriformis
(mer-mee-sa pir-ee-for-mass)

Description

These small and seemingly insignificant brown insects are very important to the environment because they aerate the soil when creating underground tunnels, they eat decaying leaves and animal, and are an essential food source within their ecosystems. So it is important we appreciate them.

Danger Factor

This genus of ant is known for their aggressive behaviour and potential to be very dangerous. Some people think their sting is delivered through their mouthpart, also known as mandibles. In fact, they use them to grip their victim while jabbing their stinger, located at the tail end of their body, into the victim multiple times, delivering a load of venom. The effect of the sting is usually pain, but it can also cause anaphylactic shock to those who are allergic, and even death. The ant's venom can paralyse smaller creatures, allowing the ant to eat them without having to hold them in place.

Conservation Status

NOT EVALUATED

Specific details around their conservation status are unknown.

They do compete with another species of ant, the black ant, and are hunted by larger animals such as wasps, spiders and birds.

Diet

The large mandibles on the front of their face assist these ants in finding dinner and carrying it back to the nest.

The larvae eat a different diet to adult ants. Adults consume nectar, fruit, seeds, honeydew and fungi, while the young eat only other smaller ants.

Location/Habitat

This species of dangerous ant lives along the eastern side of Australia in urban, woodland and eucalypt forest areas. It is relatively easy to see them once you start looking, as their mounds and quick-moving bodies are easy to spot.

Fun Facts

- The average bulldog ant only lives for approximately 9 weeks.
- These small ants can kill a human in just 15 minutes.
- They get their name, 'bulldog ant', from their aggressive behaviour.
- Bulldog ants grow wings at certain times of the year in order to fly away to find others to breed with and start their own colonies.

Myrmecia pyriformis

Rhinella marina

Cane Toad

Rhinella marina
(ri-nella mar-ina)

Description

These large amphibians can reach 10–15 centimetres long and have warts that blanket their brownish skin, although these are more common in males.

Adults have large, lumpy glands just behind their eardrums, which are known as parotid glands. These adaptations are the key to their dangerous ability to poison both humans and other animals.

Danger Factor

Cane toads are poisonous to touch but can also squirt poison on to any threats. In animals, their poison can cause a slow and painful death by shutting down the central nervous system, usually ending in cardiac arrest after just 15 minutes. In humans their poison causes temporary blindness (if it gets into the eyes) and severe pain. There have only been a few documented deaths overseas, in cases where the toads were ingested.

Conservation Status

LEAST CONCERN

The population and range of the cane toad is rapidly increasing across Australia and Hawaii, which is not good. In most areas it is considered an invasive species and there are measures in place to control its population growth, as well as to assist animals that the cane toad negatively impacts such as dingoes, freshwater crocodiles, red-bellied black snakes and others.

Cane toads face some natural predators, including animals like crows, tawny frogmouths, wolf spiders and water rats. They are also hunted for their skins which are used to make bags, souvenirs, medicines and more.

Diet

Cane toads are rarely short of food because they are not fussy eaters. In fact, they are known to eat whatever will fit in their mouths! This includes foods such as pet food, termites, ants, bees, snakes, marine snails and even other cane toads.

Location/Habitat

The cane toad was originally introduced to Australia from Hawaii in 1935 in order to control the pests that inhabited the cane fields. This is why we know it as the cane toad.

However, it is now an invasive species in Australia, as well as in many other locations including Japan, Papua New Guinea, the southern United States, tropical South America and more.

Throughout these areas, they can be found living in humid environments, typically close to humans in parks, gardens and other modified habitats.

Fun Facts

- Pet dogs are a common victim of cane toads, because they often attack, lick or eat the toads if they come into their backyards.
- There is a species of rat that is learning how to combat the cane toad. The Australian native water rat uses surgical precision to remove the toad's poisonous glands and feed on the surrounding heart or liver.

Carnivorous Caterpillar

Eupithecia
(you-pith-e-sha)

Description

At first glance, you probably think this caterpillar is like any other, spending its days feeding on plant matter in order to transition into a moth or butterfly. But this 2.5-centimetre-long creature has other plans!

Instead of chomping down on leafy greens, the carnivorous caterpillar anchors its lower legs to branches or leaves, stretches out its body and then keeps very still. The legs on its upper body are in an open position, waiting for an insect to cross its path.

Danger Factor

Although not a risk to humans, this small caterpillar is incredibly dangerous to other insects, especially when factoring in its size and evolutionary adaptation. Lucky for us, they will never evolve to human-eating size (we hope).

Conservation Status

NOT EVALUATED

Not much is known about the population size or distribution of the carnivorous caterpillar. This is most likely due to how small they are, how well they camouflage, and the fact that they are found in a relatively remote location. This means that their conservation status is not fully understood. Hopefully, research in the future will teach us more.

Diet

With a strike so fast you need a slow-motion camera to see it, the carnivorous caterpillar is an incredible predator for its size. It mimics a twig and sits in wait for an insect to trigger a hair on its back. When this happens, the caterpillar snaps back on to the insect, gripping it with their 6 front legs and securing it while it feasts – like something out of a horror movie!

Its victims include flies, crickets, moths, cockroaches and more.

Location/Habitat

Members of the *Eupithecia* genus have been found across the world, but this carnivorous species only lives on the island of Hawaii.

If you are looking for this interesting insect, you have to go to an Hawaiian forest and search under as many leaves, branches and twigs as you can.

Fun Facts

- This species of caterpillar was first documented in Hawaii in 1881.
- It is only in Hawaii that this caterpillar has become carnivorous. They have remained herbivorous everywhere else.
- It is not entirely understood why the Hawaiian *Eupithecia* made the drastic change of diet, however it is often observed that islands are hotspots for evolutionary adaptations.
- You might expect that the moths these caterpillars turn into are just as extreme, however they are average looking and have no carnivorous traits.

Eupithecia

Pan troglodytes

Chimpanzee

Pan troglodytes
(pan trog-low-die-ts)

Description

Reaching heights of approximately 1.5 metres and weights of 50 kilograms, these incredibly intelligent apes can even learn sign language! Humans share more than 98% of our DNA with these wonderful primates. In fact, the chimpanzee is more closely related to humans than it is to gorillas.

Danger Factor

Due to baby chimps' cute and playful nature, these animals are often kept as pets, both legally and illegally around the world. When they reach maturity, it becomes clear what a bad idea this is! They are very powerful creatures. In fact, a male chimp is five times as strong as a man. In the wild, it is normal for chimps to bite and be rough with one another, both during playtime and in order to assert dominance. In situations where humans are attempting to discipline them, chimpanzees have been known to bite off fingers and inflict terrible injuries, even causing death.

Conservation Status

ENDANGERED

The main dangers chimps face which cause them to be endangered are intentional poaching for their meat, being trapped in snares (sometimes meant for other animals), being captured for the pet trade, the destruction of their habitats and even occasionally being poisoned because they eat crops.

Over the years, they have also suffered from human diseases. For example, during the 1966 polio epidemic in Gombe, Nigeria, many chimpanzees became paralysed or died.

Diet

Chimpanzees are omnivorous, which means their diet is packed with a range of plants and animals, including small mammals, birds, eggs, insects, fruits, leaves, seeds, flowers and more. Their large teeth assist them in eating these foods and also help them express their emotions to one another.

Location/Habitat

Chimpanzees live in Africa, for example in countries like Tanzania and Uganda. They can be found in many different environments including tropical rainforests, dry savanna, and swamp forests. They live in groups of approximately 35 individuals, including multiple males and females, and build nests from branches and leaves every night.

Fun Facts

- They are thought to live to 50 years.
- The collective name for a group of chimps is a 'community'.
- We are so similar to chimps that we can even receive a blood transfusion from them, so long as you share the same blood type!
- Chimps have been recorded using tools to help them with tricky tasks, something very few animals do.
- Amazingly, these apes are thought to use plants for medicinal purposes. It has been observed that only the sick members of the community eat certain medicinal plants.

Coffin Ray

Hypnos monopterygius
(hip-noss monop-ter-eye-gee-us)

Description

The coffin ray needs to blend in with the seabed, so it has evolved to be a dappled grey, brown or even black shade. They reach an average length of 40 centimetres.

They have adapted something called 'spiracles', found near their eyes, which help them breathe when they are pressed against the seabed and have their gills covered.

Danger Factor

These rays use a specialised electric organ to subdue prey and defend themselves from predators. This incredible adaptation delivers a powerful shock to anything that touches the ray, sending up to 200 volts into the victim – enough to numb the impacted area! The ray's most common human victims are divers who accidentally handle or step on them. If the ray is unable to flee or hide, it has no option but to use its dangerous ability on whoever is threatening them.

Conservation Status

LEAST CONCERN

The coffin ray is quite abundant throughout its habitat and is not useful to commercial fishers. Because of this, its conservation status is 'least concern'.

These rays are occasionally captured as bycatch by trawlers. In most cases they can survive this ordeal since they can live out of water for hours at a time and are usually thrown back into the sea once found.

Diet

The coffin ray hides itself in sand on the sea floor, emerging quickly to snatch up prey such as fish, crabs and worms, before burying itself once again. Its mouth is located on the underside of its body and can stretch wide enough to consume its prey whole!

Location/Habitat

Native to Australia, coffin rays can be found around much of its coast, from warm, shallow waters at 80 metres deep to depths of 200 metres. While they are quite tricky to spot, a keen eye may find them by the raised shape of their bodies buried in the sand.

Fun Facts

- They are also called 'numb rays' and 'crampfish', because of their ability to give electric shocks.
- Some coffin rays have been found with penguins in their bellies!
- Baby coffin rays are known as 'pups'.
- When coffin rays are adults, they will have grown approximately 60 rows of teeth.

Hypnos monopterygius

Hippopotamus amphibius

Common Hippopotamus

Hippopotamus amphibius
(hippo-pot-a-mus am-fib-e-us)

Description

The hippo is one of the world's most dangerous animals due to its power and size. They can reach 4 metres in length and up to 2700 kilograms.

At birth, baby hippos already weigh around 35 kilograms!

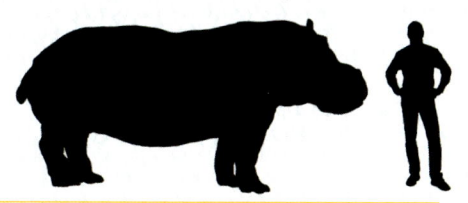

Danger Factor

Among hippos, most conflicts occur between territorial males. Usually they stop at threatening each other with a 'yawning' display, clashing their jaws and biting to show off their giant tusks. If this does not resolve the issue, their fights can end in death. Hippos are also dangerous to humans, killing approximately 500 people a year in Africa. Attacks on humans occur when hippos feel threatened and include charging, biting, dragging the victims into the water and crushing them. Be sure to admire them from a safe distance!

Conservation Status

VULNERABLE

Hippos are listed as vulnerable due to the extreme habitat loss they face and because they are hunted for their body parts. These are often used for items like jewellery, crafts and whips, and are sold on the black market.

Diet

You might think that hippos would use their 50-centimetre-long tusks for feasting on large mammals or other challenging meals. In fact, these large beasts only eat grasses, reeds and shoots. But what they do eat, they eat a lot of – approximately 40 kilograms a day!

Hippos do not use their front teeth or tusks at all during the feeding process, only during conflict. Instead, they use their muscular lips to pull on plants and transfer them to the back of the mouth where the hippos' molars do the chewing.

Location/Habitat

The common hippopotamus is quite a social creature, living in groups of 10 to 100 individuals and spending its days wallowing in lakes, wetlands and rivers, and its nights grazing. It can be found throughout sub-Saharan Africa, including Ethiopia, Kenya and Gambia.

Fun Facts

- Hippos wag their tails wildly in order to spray their droppings over a large area. This is a way of marking their territory and impressing females.
- Hippos have evolved to secrete an oily red substance from their backs, which covers them in a natural moisturiser and sunscreen and also protects them from bacteria.
- They give birth while in the water.
- Surprisingly, the hippo is closely related to ocean animals like dolphins and whales.

Crown-of-thorns Starfish

Acanthaster planci
(a-can-thast-er plan-see)

Description

Despite being called 'starfish', the crown-of-thorns starfish are not actually fish. Scientists prefer to call them 'sea stars', but their species name has not yet been officially changed. These large creatures range from 25–70 centimetres in diameter and can have between 8 and 21 arms.

Their colour ranges from red, orange, green and purple, depending on their diet.

Danger Factor

The crown-of-thorn starfish's arms feature hundreds of spines containing painful toxins. This makes for a wonderful defence mechanism. But it is not their toxicity to humans that has placed these starfish on the dangerous list. It is the danger they pose to coral reefs. They expel their stomach and wrap it around the coral, eating the tissue and leaving only the skeleton behind. In just one year, a single crown-of-thorns can destroy up to 10 square metres of precious reef, changing the ecosystems dramatically.

Conservation Status

A GLOBALLY INVASIVE SPECIES

Crown-of-thorns starfish are considered a globally invasive species. However, it is important to acknowledge that if coral reefs were not already being impacted by human-related issues, like global warming, industry pollution and overfishing, the crown-of-thorns would not be such a threat, as the ecosystem would be balanced and able to handle its normal predatory habits. It is vital we reduce the human impact on our reefs before eradicating a natural species.

Diet

Known as an opportunistic carnivore and corallivore, the crown-of-thorns starfish consumes a variety of corals and occasionally decaying sea animals. It relies on its numerous tube feet to detect its next meal.

Location/Habitat

The crown-of-thorns starfish lives in waters of the Indo-Pacific region, from the Indian Ocean all the way to the Pacific. Unfortunately, their habitats are also those that are most impacted by human activity, most notably the Great Barrier Reef off the coast of Queensland, Australia.

Fun Facts

- Despite their spiny nature, they do face some natural predators, including the giant triton snail and the titan triggerfish (featured on page 121).
- Crown-of-thorns starfish move extremely slowly, crawling just 35 centimetres per minute.
- They grow more arms as they age. Their life expectancy is up to 17 years.
- The scientific class term for sea stars/starfish is Asteroidea, so they are commonly referred to as asteroids.

Acanthaster planci

Peromyscus maniculatus

Deer Mouse

Peromyscus maniculatus
(per-o-mi-scuss man-e-cule-at-us)

Description

The deer mouse is not much different to a common house mouse. The best way to differentiate the two is through their colouring and size – deer mice have white fur on their underbelly and are around 5 centimetres longer. They reach between 11 and 22 centimetres long from head to tail and weigh just 10–24 grams.

Danger Factor

It is neither their bite nor their size that makes them dangerous. Rather, it is the fact that they can host hantavirus, which can spread to humans, causing illness. Humans can be infected by inhaling dust with particles of an infected mouse's poo, urine or saliva in it. Doing so can lead to hantavirus pulmonary syndrome, with symptoms like fever, nausea and shortness of breath. It can even lead to death. This deadly virus can be prevented from spreading by stopping deer mice from nesting in your home, and by making sure that you do not come into direct contact with them by wearing protective clothing when removing them from your home or garden.

Conservation Status

LEAST CONCERN

Due to their large population size and wide variety of habitats across North America, the deer mouse is considered of least concern.

They do, however, still face threats from predators like owls, foxes, snakes and coyotes. It is important we do not eradicate all deer mice, as they are wonderful seed dispersers, and also a popular food source for various carnivores in their ecosystem.

Diet

Deer mice are omnivorous, meaning that they eat a range of plants and animals. Their meals include small creatures like insects or parts of other small invertebrates, plant matter like flowers, seeds or fruit, and even their own poo.

Location/Habitat

Found throughout the United States, southern Canada and central and northern Mexico, the deer mouse is the most common rodent in North America.

They happily live in a number of different habitats, including swamps, woodlands, deserts, and agricultural fields. It is when they live in close proximity to humans, for example nesting in the roofs and walls of homes, that they become dangerous.

Fun Facts

- Baby deer mice, known as 'pups', are small, hairless and pink when born, and do not open their eyes for approximately 15 days.
- They enter a state of sleep, known as torpor, in winter. In torpor, they decrease their body temperature, heart rate and energy. This is useful in helping them survive the cold months.
- Deer mice are known to eat their own poo. They most likely do this to absorb nutrients which were lost the first time around.

Electric Eel

Electrophorus voltai
(elec-tro-for-us volt-eye)

Description

Although these animals are called eels, they are technically a type of knifefish. They get their name because of their close resemblance to eels. These fish can grow to lengths of 2.5 metres and weigh up 20 kilograms, with approximately 80% of their insides being made up of their electrical organs. To protect themselves from their own electricity, they have evolved a thick oily substance that covers their body.

Danger Factor

Electric eels can impart a shock of up to 860 volts and have been recorded to kill humans through heart and respiratory failure, although many of those victims had pre-existing heart conditions. They only inflict their large electric discharge when feeling threatened or trying to hunt as doing so helps them locate their food.

Conservation Status

LEAST CONCERN

There are many electric eels distributed across a wide range of habitats. This, combined with the fact that they have few predators, makes them of least concern when it comes to conservation.

Specimens are occasionally collected for the pet trade, scientific research and for human consumption. Fortunately, this has very little impact on their population size.

Diet

Electric eels use a weak, internal electric organ to locate their prey. Once found, they will stun their dinner with a larger electrical current, then suction the immobilised fish or small mammals into their mouths.

Location/Habitat

These unusual fish live in the Orinoco and Guyana rivers and in the Amazon River basin in South America. With their dark, muddy colours, they blend into swamps, streams and riverbeds, hiding in the shadows.

Fun Facts

- They are nocturnal creatures, meaning they sleep during the day and are active at night.
- Rather than laying a typical batch of eggs, the female deposits her eggs into a foam nest that the male eel creates with his saliva.
- Surprisingly, electric eels can breathe air and take in 80% of their oxygen by regularly swimming to the surface and taking a breath.
- Newly hatched baby eels often eat their siblings who are slower to hatch.
- It is thought electric eels can live for between 10 and 22 years.

Electrophorus voltai

Metasepia pfefferi

Flamboyant Cuttlefish

Metasepia pfefferi
(met-a-sep-e-a feff-er-e)

Description

The flamboyant cuttlefish can change colour because they have chromatophores. These are cells that both reflect light and contain pigment and can actually create a moving colour display on their skin. This magnificent act of colour change on this 6–8-centimetre-long cephalopod occurs for a number of reasons, for example when luring in prey or deterring predators, as it acts as a warning sign that they should not be messed with. Typically, however, they are much duller, allowing them to blend in with their environment.

Danger Factor

Just like the southern blue-ringed octopus on page 113, the flamboyant cuttlefish is considered lethal to other sea creatures and potentially humans, because they are poisonous. If consumed by other marine life, they will most likely cause tremendous pain, paralysis, respiratory failure and death. However, it is not yet fully understood what its toxin, called tetrodotoxin, would do to a human. Research teams in the United States are currently conducting studies to better understand the toxicology of this little cephalopod.

Conservation Status

DATA DEFICIENT

More information is needed in order to assess the conservation status of the flamboyant cuttlefish. It is thought, however, that the potential threats they do face include being captured for the aquarium trade and increasing ocean acidity caused by global warming.

Diet

They spend their days searching for prey, either stalking them or luring them in with their bright colours, eventually finding crustaceans such as grass shrimp and bony fish to snack on.

Location/Habitat

Found across the Indo-Pacific oceans, the flamboyant cuttlefish lives on sandy and muddy sea floors around the coasts of western and northern Australia, Indonesia and the southern side of New Guinea. Although they can be found at depths ranging from 3–86 metres, they prefer shallow, tropical waters where they will often 'walk' along the seabed.

Fun Facts

- The time it takes for their eggs to hatch depends on the temperature of the water.
- Flamboyant cuttlefish are thought to live 1.5–2 years.
- The female cuttlefish lays her eggs slowly in order to find a hiding spot (such as behind rocks or in crevices) for each one.
- The white, chalky back end of cuttlefish, known as a 'cuttlebone', is often spotted washed up on beaches. These are given to pet birds as they are packed with calcium and help strengthen the birds' beaks.

Geography Cone Snail

Conus geographus
(cone-us geog-raf-us)

Description

The geography cone snail is a species of gastropod and, like other gastropods, it uses a large, flat body part known as a 'foot' to help it travel along the ground. They can grow to approximately 15 centimetres long! Of the 500 known cone snail species, the geography cone is the most venomous.

Danger Factor

What makes the geography cone snail so deadly is its ability to deliver concentrated doses of dangerous toxins through its extendable, hollow tooth which sits inside a proboscis, a long tubular organ seen in the illustration. This is often referred to as a 'harpoon'.

Although a geography cone's sting can feel as mild as a bee sting, it is certainly much more dangerous. For humans, it can cause respiratory paralysis and even death within just one hour. The reason behind its near painless sting is that its venom also holds pain-killing properties. These have been found to be 10,000 times more effective than morphine. The venom in one sting can kill up to 15 people.

Conservation Status

LEAST CONCERN

This species of cone snail is common in a wide range of locations and fortunately faces very few threats due to its highly venomous nature, making it of least concern within the conservation world. However, other marine creatures like crabs have been known to kill geography cones by using their strong claws to crack open their shells. Another threat they face is from humans collecting and selling them in trade markets for their magnificent shells.

Diet

The geography cone snail uses its harpoon to hunt a range of prey, such as small fish, other snails and marine worms. Sensing the food nearby, it shoots its tooth out from inside the proboscis and injects its prey with paralysing venom. It then swallows it whole.

Location/Habitat

To come across a geography cone snail, you will need to be swimming in coral reefs or shallow waters around sandy areas in the Indo-Pacific region. This includes locations on the coasts of Australia, such as Darwin and Brisbane, as well as New Caledonia.

Fun Facts

- An antivenom does not exist for geography cone snails. The only solution is to attempt to remove the existing toxins, or to prevent them from spreading until they wear off.
- Geography cone snails can live to the ripe old age of 15 years.
- In the United States, these animals are occasionally used as an ingredient in medicines for people with schizophrenia.

Conus geographus

Blattella germanica

German Cockroach

Blattella germanica
(blat-tella germ-ani-ca)

Description

With around 4500 species of cockroach in the world and 450 of those species living in Australia, there is one which stands out for its invasive behaviour and ability to be dangerous. It is the German cockroach.

At just 1.6 centimetres long, it is easily identified by two dark stripes on either side of its upper back, which is known as a pronotum.

Danger Factor

It is not the German cockroach's bite or sting that is so dangerous, but rather its habit of contaminating the foods and surfaces it comes in contact with. These cockroaches can carry E. coli and salmonella, which can cause bacterial diseases. They also drop faeces and layers of skin which can trigger asthma attacks.

Conservation Status

NOT EVALUATED

Due to the German cockroach's ability to reproduce incredibly fast, the fact that they have few predators, and can go unnoticed in any nook or cranny, they have a high population size, which is rapidly increasing. Their conservation status is not known, but they are considered a nuisance by most people.

Diet

They are not fussy when it comes to their diet, feasting on a variety of foods including rice, potatoes, cereal, meat, seeds and in some cases even toothpaste!

Location/Habitat

Unlike its name suggests, the German cockroach is originally from Africa, but it can now be found across the globe. They enjoy warm, tropical climates and prefer to be in the dark and out of sight of passers-by. They can be found near food sources, whether that be in drains or in houses.

Fun Facts

- Despite their small size, they are speedier than most other species of cockroach.
- One of the reasons they can so quickly infest an area is their speedy reproduction rate. They can lay up to 40 eggs at a time.
- Although the adult German cockroach has evolved wings, they almost never fly.
- They can live for up to 200 days.
- German cockroaches are considered one of the smallest pest species ever.

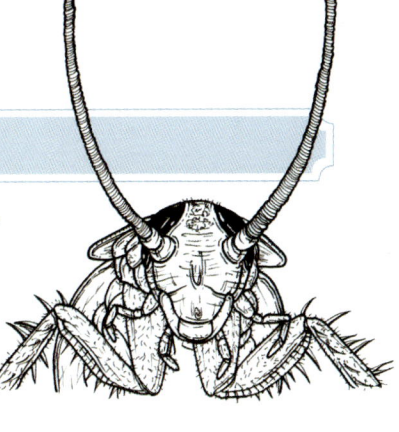

Giant Otter

Pteronura brasiliensis
(terro-new-ra bra-sil-e-en-sis)

Description

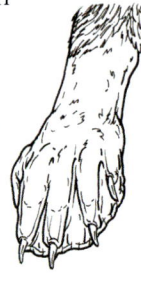

Winning the title for the largest otter in the world, the giant otter weighs in at 34 kilograms and is 1.8 metres tall on average. They have water-repellent fur, webbed feet, strong tails, and ears and noses that close when submerged.

The giant otter is closely related to the wolverine, found on page 125. They belong to the same family, known as the Mustelidae family, and share similar features.

Danger Factor

These carnivorous members of the weasel family are extremely territorial and can be very feisty when something threatens them or their young. Utilising their sharp teeth, powerful jaws and intimidating claws, they will tear into predators and even humans. They have been documented taking on some of the most feared animals in the world, such as the caiman, piranha and anaconda. Luckily, humans are not their desired meal and they have no interest in us unless we pose a threat, so we can rest easy. But it is important to maintain a respectful distance of these otters or you could face a feisty attack.

Conservation Status

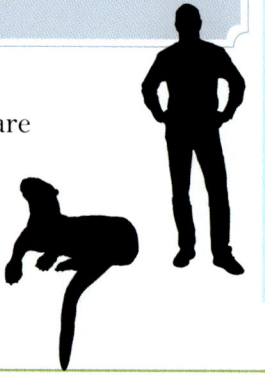

ENDANGERED

The habitats of the giant otter are being destroyed at an alarming rate, so much so that it is thought their population size will decrease by 50% or more by 2045. They are impacted by pollutants in the water, diseases of the animal kingdom, and fishers who see them as competitors for fish. They have also been killed for their skins in the past.

Diet

Due to the muddy, unclear waters in which they live, giant otters must rely not only on their vision to find prey, but also their sense of smell, hearing and touch. Using their sharp teeth, the giant otter will feast predominantly on fish (catfish to be precise), but has also been found eating turtles and snakes. After capturing their victim, they swim to the surface or to land to feed.

Location/Habitat

Endemic to South America, the giant otter can be found in streams, rivers, creeks, swamps and lakes. Their ideal habitat is in large, slow-moving bodies of water. You will most likely see them in the Amazon, Orinoco and La Plata River systems, in groups of approximately 2–15 individuals, including a variety of adults and young.

Fun Facts

- Giant otters live for 10–13 years.
- They have unique light brown markings on their chests which help them identify one another.
- The collective noun for otters in water is a 'raft'.
- Giant otters are apex predators, however, on rare occasions, they have been seen succumbing to pumas and jaguars.
- Science suggests that these otters were even larger once, reaching 2.4 metres! Due to their declining population, these large specimens no longer exist.

Pteronura brasiliensis

Heloderma suspectum

Gila Monster

Heloderma suspectum
(hello-derma sus-pect-um)

Description

The Gila monster (pronounced hee-la) is one of just two venomous lizards in the world. It is covered from head to tail in small, bead-like scales ranging in colour from black, orange, yellow and pink, and can reach lengths of up to 60 centimetres.

Danger Factor

Despite its 'dangerous' label, the Gila monster is actually rather docile and placid by nature. However, if you get too close and are bitten you are in store for a lot of pain! The venom which these lizards produce from glands in their jaws can have quite uncomfortable effects, including dizziness, diarrhoea, vomiting, swelling and, if not treated correctly, infection. The Gila monster will bite down to release its venom and perform a chewing-like movement to pump out more. Often, it will refuse to let go and will need to be forcibly removed from the body.

Conservation Status

NEAR THREATENED

This unique and dangerous creature is struggling, its population falling in the face of continuous threats. The majority of the dangers these lizards face are due to human activities. For example, they are poached for the pet trade or killed because of their venomous nature. They are also threatened through the clearing of their habitats in order to build roads, buildings and other developments.

Diet

Impressively, these small lizards are actually quite hardy when it comes to feeding, as they can survive on only 4 or 5 meals a year! When they do eat, they enjoy feasting on rats, rabbits, other lizards, as well as snake and bird eggs. They use their forked tongues to taste the air and through this, find their prey.

They rarely use their venom to kill their prey, suggesting that this adaptation is mainly for defence.

Location/Habitat

These bumpy lizards can be found in north-western Mexico and the south-western United States, including locations such as California, south Arizona and south-west Utah.

They live in rocky and mountainous desert environments, often hiding underground or seeking shelter during the hottest part of the day, and spending up to 98% of their time concealed from view.

Fun Facts

- Another name for this lizard is 'escorpion'.
- Although in captivity they can live up to 20 years, in the wild they will typically reach just 8 years old.
- The collective noun for a group of these lizards is a 'lounge'.
- The Gila monster is immune to its own venom.
- The small bumps underneath their scales are actually bone!

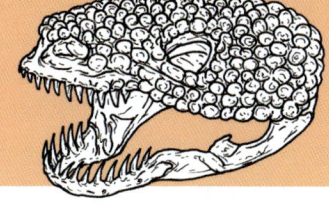

Golden Poison Frog

Phyllobates terribilis
(fill-o-bates ter-i-bil-us)

Description

The golden poison frog's vibrant colour acts as a warning to predators, letting them know that this 5-centimetre-long animal is very dangerous. Over time, some poisonous, venomous and downright dangerous animals developed vibrant shades of yellow, green, blue and red. Predators eventually associated the hazard with these colours and learnt to stay clear; this is now known as aposematic colouration.

Danger Factor

Golden poison frogs contain the same toxins as the hooded pitohui on page 70, and a single frog can kill 10 men. They secrete their poison through glands on their skin, and just touching the frog can cause a severe burning sensation for hours. If this poison enters the bloodstream, it can cause heart failure. In the past, tribes in South America have wiped this frog's poison on to their blowgun darts, using this to help hunt small animals. This is how they got the name 'poison dart frog'. It is actually from eating a small species of beetle known as a melyrid beetle that these frogs source their dangerous abilities. These insects are packed with toxins called batrachotoxins, and they will build up in the frogs over time, eventually seeping through their pores and inflicting the agony.

Conservation Status

ENDANGERED

The golden poison frog is considered endangered because of the many human-related threats it faces. These include habitat destruction, the use of pesticide and even poaching for the pet trade. Fortunately for them, they face very few natural predators because of their toxic nature.

Diet

They use their long, sticky tongues to feed on creatures such as ants, termites, crickets, flies and beetles.

Location/Habitat

They are endemic to the Amazon rainforest along the Pacific coast of Colombia, which receives up to 5 metres of rain a year.

Due to its bright colouring, the golden poison frog can be somewhat easily spotted among the leaves and on the forest floor. They need very humid habitats, as the mixture of heat and moisture is essential for their survival.

Fun Facts

- When they are collected and kept in captivity for a long period of time, these frogs lose their toxicity. This is because they are no longer eating the melyrid beetle which gives them their poison.
- The collective name for a group of frogs is an 'army'.
- In this species, the males store the eggs on their backs until they can safely deliver them to the fertilisation site in the water.

Phyllobates terribilis

Hydrocynus goliath

Goliath Tigerfish

Hydrocynus goliath
(hydro-sigh-nus go-lie-ath)

Description

The goliath tigerfish is the largest of all tigerfish species, weighing in at around 50 kilograms and measuring 1.5 metres long. Their huge size is how they get their name.

They are often compared to piranhas, featured on page 95. As well as their size and the fact that they do not hunt in packs, both fish have similar, interlocking teeth and a ferocious nature.

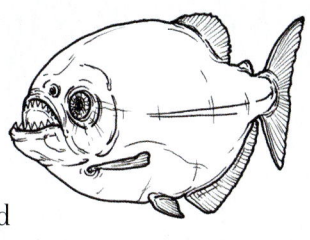

Danger Factor

Goliath tigerfish have 32 enormous teeth which measure up to 2.5 centimetres long and are sharp enough to slice a fish clean in half. Humans are not out of danger, and there have been a small number of recorded attacks over the years. Because of this, it is important that we recognise the goliath tigerfish's strength and do not go out searching to catch one.

Conservation Status

LEAST CONCERN

Due to this fish's size and aggressive nature, it faces very few natural threats. It does, however, face human-related threats through fishing. These fish are caught for both food and as trophies. To maintain their population and position within the ecosystem, it is important that we release these magnificent fish or do not fish them at all.

Diet

Using their ability to sense vibrations through the water as well as their great eyesight, goliath tigerfish hunt in rough waters where their prey will be too exhausted and distracted to flee from their oncoming jaws.

Location/Habitat

Found throughout central Africa, the goliath tigerfish dwells in lakes and large rivers, primarily within the Congo River basin.

Fun Facts

- Unlike other fish in African waters, this species does not fear crocodiles. There are rumours that they even eat small ones!
- They can live for up to 15 years in captivity.
- This astonishing fish gained a lot of media attention when it was featured on the television program *River Monsters* in 2010. It took a 91-kilogram rod and an 8-hour struggle before the fisher was able to capture a goliath tigerfish. The fish was injured during the struggle and was not able to be released back into the wild, so it was given to local villagers.

Greater Slow Loris

Nycticebus coucang
(nik-tis-bus cow-kang)

Description

The greater slow loris is a small primate, which only grows to approximately 35 centimetres and weighs around 600 grams. It has thick fur, small ears and large eyes which help it see in the dark.

Danger Factor

Despite its innocent appearance, the greater slow loris is actually quite toxic! Like all slow loris species, it produces toxin in glands inside its elbows. It spreads this through its fur by licking its elbows, mixing the toxin with its saliva, and then brushing it through its fur using its toothcomb. A toothcomb is a special group of front teeth which helps some mammals groom themselves. The oil that results from the mixing of saliva and toxin is powerful enough to cause anaphylactic shock or even kill a human if they are not treated. But for a human to be injured by a slow loris, they must either be bitten by one, or eat one, both of which are highly unlikely.

Conservation Status

VULNERABLE

Unfortunately, the greater slow loris faces many threats. Their habitats are being cleared, their body parts are used for traditional medicine, and they also face natural predators like pythons, orangutans and eagles.

Diet

Greater slow lorises are nocturnal and arboreal, meaning they spend their time up in the trees. They spend their nights foraging and feeding on a range of foods including nectar, sap and gums. A small portion of their diet is also made up of fruit, insects, spiders, eggs and snails.

Location/Habitat

Although these primates are only active at night, it is possible to see them in the wild. They live up in the trees and rely on their amazing climbing ability and grip to crawl from branch to branch in a variety of forests and swamps in Malaysia, Indonesia, Singapore and parts of Thailand.

Fun Facts

- Mother slow lorises will lick their babies and cover them in their own toxic oil in order to protect them from predators.
- The action in which they pee while moving is known as 'rhythmic urination'.
- They are known by locals as 'malu-malu' which means 'shy' in Indonesian.
- Researchers are now using a special red light when out in the field in order to protect the slow loris' sensitive eyes.

Nycticebus coucang

Trachinus draco

Greater Weever Fish

Trachinus draco
(track-i-nuss dray-co)

Description

The greater weever fish is a somewhat typical looking fish. It has a long body that is dappled with brown and orange patterns and an upturned mouth. It reaches just 25 centimetres on average.

Danger Factor

Greater weever fish have a row of needle-like spines down their back and on their gill covers which secrete a venomous discharge. This venom is so strong that it can cause serious injury or death for humans. Some of the early signs that you have been stung include sharp pain, an intense burning sensation, nausea, headaches, fainting and seizures. In order to avoid being stung, do not handle the fish if you catch one. Instead, cut the line and release it back into the water.

Conservation Status

LEAST CONCERN

Quite abundant and widespread within their habitats, the greater weever fish is considered of least concern. However, it still faces threats through the fishing trade. These fish are caught both intentionally and as bycatch by trawlers.

Despite its venomous nature, the greater weever fish is still relatively valuable to fish markets, where its spines are removed and it is sold for human consumption and as fish bait in southern Europe and Scandinavia.

Diet

The greater weever fish is nocturnal, meaning that it is active at night and sleeps or hides away during the day. It spends its nights feeding on other fish and small invertebrates.

Location/Habitat

Greater weever fish will hide their flat bodies by resting on the seabed, buried up to their eyes and dorsal fin. Through this, they are able to protect themselves from predators. These fish reside in depths of approximately 100 metres and are not often seen by swimmers or fishers, but those who are unlucky enough to step on one will find themselves in trouble. The regions that they reside in extend from Morocco to Mauritania, the Canary Islands and Madeira, as well as Norway, the Mediterranean Sea and the Black Sea.

Fun Facts

- There are 9 different species of weever fish.
- Their name 'weever' originates from the Old French word 'wivre' which means 'dragon'.
- The oldest greater weever fish lived for 14 years!
- Weever fish species are known to be some of the most venomous species in the temperate zone.
- They can reach a whopping 50 centimetres in length, double their average!

Hooded Pitohui

Pitohui dichrous
(pit-o-hoo-ee die-cr-ow-s)

Description

Using the same evolutionary adaptations as the golden poison frog on page 62, the hooded pitohui is coloured black and orange in order to warn predators that it should not be eaten. Their deep red eyes and powerful beaks draw similarities to crows and ravens, as they are closely related and are all members of the Corvidae family.

Danger Factor

One would not expect this small bird to be of any threat to anything other than some passing insects or hanging fruit. After all, they are just 23 centimetres tall and weigh only 65 grams. Despite their unthreatening appearance, they are in fact the most poisonous bird in the world, with toxins settling in their feathers and skin. The toxin causes an unpleasant tingling, burning and numbing effect on any human that touches them. In rare cases, exposure can even cause heart failure. By eating a small species of melyrid beetle packed with batrachotoxins, this pitohui is able to collect the toxins in its own body. The more of them it eats, the more toxic the pitohui is.

Conservation Status

LEAST CONCERN

Fortunately, the hooded pitohui faces no immediate threats and its population is abundant. However, since it lives in forests, there is potential for its habitats to be affected by industries like logging, mining, and farming.

Diet

This species of bird lives off seeds, fruit and insects. Its diet actually affects its ability to emit dangerous toxins. If the hooded pitohui doesn't eat the melyrid beetle, it isn't poisonous so the beetle is essential to its protection against predators.

Location/Habitat

The hooded pitohui is native to New Guinea, enjoying warmer climates that are surrounded by rainforest and forest environments. They are social birds and often associate with different species during foraging sessions.

Fun Facts

- These birds rely on their vibrant colouring and distinct odour to warn any potential threats that they are not to be messed with.
- There are birds who have evolved a similar colouring to the pitohui, but who do not contain dangerous toxins. Instead they rely on predators mistaking them for hooded pitohui and steering clear.
- Some locals still eat the pitohui, however it must first be carefully prepared in order to remove all its toxin-containing parts.
- The hooded pitohui was one of the first birds ever recorded to be poisonous.

Pitohui dichrous

Dermatobia hominis

Human Botfly

Dermatobia hominis
(derma-toby-a hom-in-is)

Description

These small flies, which grow to 1–2 centimetres, are often said to look like bumble bees. However, these insects are much more disturbing and can be even more dangerous.

The females of this species are typically larger than the males, and have eyes which are situated further apart, making them sexually dimorphic.

Danger Factor

The botfly is so dangerous because it has the ability to live within human/animal skin and cause severe infection. Without proper treatment it can cause death. They lay their eggs on skin and the larvae then digs themselves into their victims, usually through existing abrasions. This infestation of the body of a living host is known as myiasis and is the reason such harm is caused to the victims. The larvae will continue to live within this safe environment for up to 1–2 months, until they are ready to emerge as maggots. The best thing to do if you have a botfly larva inside you is either leave it until it is ready to emerge naturally, or block off its air supply by covering the area and patiently wait for it to die.

Conservation Status

NOT EVALUATED

The conservation status of the human botfly is yet to be evaluated. They are considered quite the nuisance for both humans and animals because they can infest an animal with thousands of maggots at a time. There are records of these insects stopping herding operations in the cattle industry of Central America.

Diet

Due to their incredibly short lives, adult human botflies do not actually eat.

However, the larvae feast on the flesh of the mammals they live inside, usually on the subcutaneous or innermost layer of the skin. This gives them enough energy for adulthood.

Location/Habitat

These flies are endemic to South and Central America. They are found in humid, tropical and semi-tropical forest-like environments.

Although the human botfly is not native to many other countries, it is sometimes accidentally transported inside the bodies of tourists.

Fun Facts

- A traditional method of treating a botfly infestation is to cover the area with the sap of a native tree, the matatorsalo.
- The term 'bot' means 'maggot'.
- If these insects are punctured while inside the body, their bodily fluids can cause anaphylactic shock!
- Females can lay up to 1000 eggs.

Indian Red Scorpion

Hottentotta tamulus
(hot-ten-tota tam-u-lus)

Description

The scorpion is actually an arachnid, meaning that these animals are in the same family as spiders! You can see the similarity in that both scorpions and spiders have 8 legs and 2 body segments. They also share a reputation for being two of the most feared animals by society.

Danger Factor

Although they reach just 7.5 centimetres long, the Indian red scorpion is extremely dangerous and has been known to kill. Those at most risk are typically children, as they are small and will often walk around without shoes on and play in areas where the scorpion is abundant. However, adults are also at risk and should remain alert. While these animals do not target humans specifically, they will sting when they feel threatened. Even a child's foot would look pretty large and threatening to a scorpion! Symptoms of their sting include vomiting, increased heart rate and potential anaphylaxis.

Conservation Status

NOT EVALUATED

Not much is known about the population size or conservation status of the Indian red scorpion.

They are thought to be plentiful despite being a snack for many species of bird and suffering from human poaching for the pet trade.

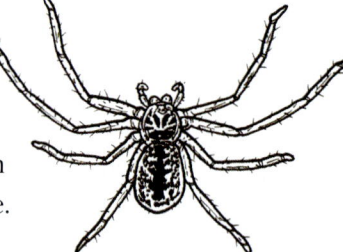

Diet

These carnivorous creatures rely on vibration to find their prey, jumping onto critters like insects and lizards, sometimes even feasting on rats.

They do not always use their stingers to kill as they can often rely on their pincers to grip the victim while their digestive fluids turn its insides into liquid. They then suck out these innards, leaving the outside intact.

Location/Habitat

Like its name suggests, the Indian red scorpion is found in India. They are also found in areas of Nepal, Pakistan and Sri Lanka. They often hide under rocks or other surfaces because they enjoy the dark.

One of the main reasons these creatures cause so many fatalities is because they live in close proximity to humans.

Fun Facts

- Baby scorpions are called 'scorplings'.
- Under a black light, the Indian red scorpion is actually fluorescent!
- During their mating rituals, male scorpions grab on to the female's pincers and dance around.
- These scorpions can live for 5 years in captivity, but usually not quite as long in the wild.
- There are around 1000 species of scorpion and it is thought that the Indian red scorpion is the most toxic.

Hottentotta tamulus

Carukia barnesi

Irukandji Jellyfish

Carukia barnesi
(car-oo-kia bar-nes-e)

Description

Many people are surprised to learn there are over 25 species of box jellyfish living in the ocean, with the Irukandji jellyfish being one of the most deadly. As small as 25 millimetres in diameter with tentacles reaching 1 metre, the Irukandji jellyfish is almost invisible to the average person.

Danger Factor

Irukandji jellyfish are incredibly dangerous, they even have their own syndrome named after them, the Irukandji syndrome, which outlines the expected symptoms one can have after being stung. Beginning with just a mosquito bite sensation, it soon causes excruciating pain throughout the body, nausea, headaches and increased heart rate. It can also lead to fluid entering the lungs as well as brain haemorrhages. These animals send up to 100 people to hospital every year and due to their miniscule size, it is difficult to avoid being stung; the only solution is to not swim in their habitats at all.

Conservation Status

NOT EVALUATED

There is still much to be learnt about the Irukandji jellyfish, including their conservation status. It is difficult to find out more about them due to the vastness of the ocean and their small size, however they are incredibly interesting creatures and have intrigued scientists all over the world.

Diet

Their method for catching and killing prey is quite gruesome. The jellyfish will find nearby fish, shrimp and other sea creatures and release a harpoon-like coil full of toxins, out of a tentacle. These toxins are injected into the prey, rendering it immobile. The jellyfish will then use their long tentacles to bring back the meal and consume it.

Location/Habitat

This small but deadly jellyfish is found along the northern Australian coastline, from Broome in Western Australia all the way across to Rockhampton in Queensland. In locations like the Great Barrier Reef, they will spend their time in deep waters out of sight.

Fun Facts

- So little is known about the Irukandji jellyfish that researchers are still unsure how long they can live.
- They are sometimes referred to as the 'invisible danger' because of their small size and transparent nature.
- Although these creatures don't have brains, they do have eyes!
- There is still no antivenom for this species.
- One surviving victim spent two days in a coma after being stung.

Kissing Bug

Triatoma dimidiata
(try-a-toe-ma dim-e-di-ata)

Description

In just the United States, there are 11 different species of kissing bug, all of which have the ability to be dangerous.

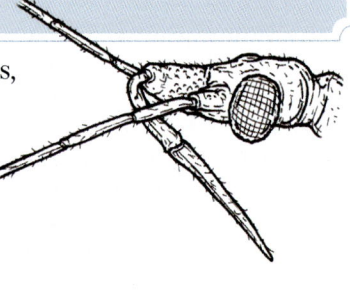

The majority of species are dark brown with a striped orange band around the edge of their bodies and range from 2–3 centimetres in size. Their long unusual mouthparts are distinctive and give them the nickname 'cone-nose bug'.

Danger Factor

While it might look and sound fairly innocent, the kissing bug has a not so sweet habit that makes it dangerous. Through its mouthpart it sucks blood from its victim's face. This is how it gets the name 'kissing bug'. Waiting until their prey is asleep, the kissing bug finds the eye region of a victim and sucks their blood. People who are allergic to these insects can experience anaphylaxis, which causes difficulty breathing and a drop in blood pressure. More often, kissing bugs will pass on a disease called Chagas disease. This can cause fever, headaches and swollen lymph nodes. In severe cases, it can lead to an enlarged heart, an irregular heartbeat and other dangerous symptoms. If not treated, it is potentially fatal. The good news is, not all kissing bugs carry this dangerous disease.

Conservation Status

NOT EVALUATED

Kissing bugs are preyed on by animals such as lizards, rats, chickens and toads. There are also species of spider and wasp that eat young kissing bugs. Others lay their eggs in the adults. This is a form of parasitism and is somewhat ironic, since the kissing bug is considered a parasite itself.

Diet

The diet of kissing bugs is quite simple, they are parasitic and spend the night feeding predominantly on their host's blood. Typically found on animals like dogs and foxes, they can also feed on humans. More recently, they have been documented eating plants.

Location/Habitat

The infamous kissing bug lives across areas of South and Central America, including in Peru, Mexico, Costa Rica and Colombia.

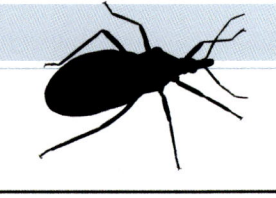

25-30 millimetres

Depending on the variety of hosts nearby, they can be found in rock piles or tree hollows in rainforest-like environments.

Fun Facts
- They have very flat bodies before feeding and become quite engorged afterwards.
- It is thought the kissing bug can live to 3 years of age.
- In this species, the female is larger than the male, making them sexually dimorphic.

Triatoma dimidiata

Varanus komodoensis

Komodo Dragon

Varanus komodoensis
(var-a-nus komo-do-en-sis)

Description

The Komodo dragon has evolved over millions of years to reach lengths of 2.6 metres and weights of 80 kilograms, making it the largest lizard in the world. While its 60 serrated teeth are just 1 centimetre long and can be difficult to see, they nonetheless cause a lot of damage.

Danger Factor

The truly haunting aspect of the Komodo dragon, and the thing which makes it so dangerous, is its patient nature. If the Komodo cannot subdue a bitten victim straight away, it will stalk the wounded animal for hours, sometimes even days, until its prey eventually dies from the many toxins and bacteria within the Komodo's saliva. This saliva, paired with its serrated teeth and powerful body, means that it can injure and kill almost all animals around it.

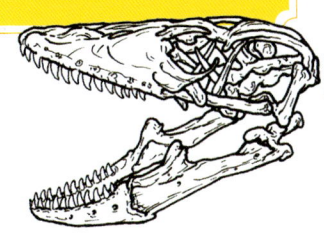

Humans are not much different, falling victim to Komodo bites, cuts and thrashing attacks over the years. Komodo dragons have attacked around 24 people since the 1970s, killing 5.

Conservation Status

VULNERABLE

Although the Komodo dragon has few natural predators, it is still listed as vulnerable and, if not helped soon, it faces the threat of extinction. Due to hunting and poaching, and human settlements encroaching on their native habitats, there are only 3000–5000 left.

Diet

Komodos dominate other species in their habitats and are known to consume a wide range of animals, including pigs, deer, water buffalo and horses. However, they prefer to scavenge and usually eat the decaying leftovers of other creatures' kills. The males eat first, then females and juveniles, after which there is almost nothing left.

Location/Habitat

These days, Komodo dragons are found on just a small collection of islands in Indonesia including Rintja and Komodo. Young Komodos spend the first few months of their lives up in the trees in order to avoid predators and stay out of sight.

The adults, on the other hand, are much easier to spot and can be found on the ground in open woodlands around dry riverbeds. Because they are cold-blooded, they usually retreat to burrows and nests at night in order to stay warm.

Fun Facts

- Males use their strong tails to stand on their hind legs and fight off other competing males.
- They are nicknamed 'land crocodile' by locals.
- They have a long, forked tongue which they use to taste the air and can recognise smells up to 8 kilometres away.
- Female Komodo dragons have been known to create decoy nests in order to lead predators astray.

Leopard Seal

Hydrurga leptonyx
(hi-drurg-a lep-ton-ix)

Description

The leopard seal is a top predator within its habitat. Its slender, powerful and streamlined body allows it to dart through the water at impressive speeds, while also playfully twisting and flipping. They have large front flippers, each with webbed digits, and an enormous mouth full of sharp teeth. At lengths of 2.8–3.8 metres and weights of 260–500 kilograms, the leopard seal is the second largest species of seal in Antarctica, losing only to the enormous southern elephant seal.

Danger Factor

Like its name suggests, the leopard seal has some similarities in appearance and behaviour to a certain feisty big cat. It uses its large, powerful teeth to tear apart its prey, often playing with it before eating it. Unfortunately, in 2003 a leopard seal even killed a British scientist, though it is unclear whether this was an accident or on purpose. In most cases, however, these elusive seals will treat divers, photographers and scientists with curiosity and playfulness, so it is important we do not judge them prematurely.

Conservation Status

LEAST CONCERN

Despite the fact that the leopard seal's population seems large and stable, there are concerns about what effect global warming will have. The seal's habitats are made up of predominantly sea ice and are at risk of melting as the earth gets hotter. Increased tourism, boat activity and fishing are also potential threats.

Diet

The leopard seal's diet varies depending on the season and abundance of prey in the area. They can be found eating krill, squid, fish, penguins, birds and even other seals.

Location/Habitat

Found only in the southern hemisphere, leopard seals live in the Antarctic and sub-Antarctic waters. When not in the water, they prefer to lay on sheets of floating ice. They are skilled swimmers and divers, and one seal was even recorded at depths of 304 metres.

FUN FACTS

- It is thought that leopard seals can live for over 26 years.
- Their scientific name, *Hydrurga leptonyx*, translates to 'slender-clawed water-worker'.
- When born, leopard seal pups weigh a hefty 30–35 kilograms and measure up to 1.6 metres long.
- Their whiskers are so sensitive that even in dark, murky water, they can sense the difference between large and small fish, knowing which ones are worth their pursuit.
- They are considered apex predators in Antarctica, with only killer whales posing a potential threat.

Hydrurga leptonyx

Alces americanus

Moose

Alces americanus
(al-ces am-eri-carn-us)

Description

With the loose skin hanging from underneath their chin (known as a 'bell'), their long and large nose, enormous antlers and lengthy legs, the moose is a very striking animal. Certainly not one you would easily miss! The largest moose on record reached a height of 2 metres and weighed 600 kilograms. They rely on their sharp hooves to kick anything that poses a threat but do this mostly to protect their calves.

Danger Factor

Due to the large range and population size of the moose, attacks on humans are not unusual. In Alaska alone, 5-10 people are injured each year. That is more than the number of bear attacks. They become aggressive when food is scarce, during the mating season and when protecting their young. Attacks include charging, kicking and stomping, all of which are incredibly dangerous when factoring in their enormous size. The best thing to do if a moose is coming after you is to hide behind something solid like a tree and remain still.

Conservation Status

LEAST CONCERN

Fortunately, the moose is abundant throughout their ever-growing range. Even so, they do face some threats and are frequently hunted or preyed on by bears and wolves. Their habitats are also being altered through human action.

Diet

The moose is known to feed on a variety of plants, which is why it has historically been seen as a pest by local farmers. However, when they are not close to farms, they like to eat different species of shrubs and trees, including willow, birch, juniper and blueberry.

Location/Habitat

As you might have gathered from their scientific name, the moose is from America, North America to be specific. They can be found in areas like the northern Great Lakes, Rocky Mountains, Canada and Alaska, where they enjoy spending their days in forests, woodlands and lowland mountains.

Fun Facts

- They can live up to 20 years.
- Moose enjoy mineral licks – naturally occurring pockets of salt and various minerals that help them stay nourished.
- The name 'moose' is derived from the term 'moosh', which means 'eater' and 'stripper of bark' to the traditional owners of the land.
- Moose are excellent swimmers.
- The 'velvet' which grows on the antlers of moose and other mammals is blood-engorged skin that sheds every year.

Mosaic Crab

Lophozozymus pictor
(lof-o-zoz-eye-mus pic-tor)

Description

The mosaic crab receives its name from the beautiful mosaic-like patterns found across its body. It has eight legs littered with small hairs and two black pincers at the front. Many of the toxic crab species also have black coloured pincers, possibly suggesting danger to predators. The width of these crabs reach just 10 centimetres.

Danger Factor

This small crab does not look more dangerous than any other species, however it contains toxins that are so powerful they can even kill a human. Similar to the golden poison frog on page 62, the mosaic crab obtains its toxins from the food it eats. It feeds on a type of poisonous sea cucumber and the toxins slowly multiply in the crab's body, making it especially dangerous for anything unfortunate enough to eat it.

In some species, cooking the meat will make it safe to eat, but not with mosaic crabs. Humans who ingest cooked or uncooked mosaic crabs may become paralysed in parts of their body. They have even been the cause of several deaths.

Conservation Status

NOT EVALUATED

The conservation status of the mosaic crab is not known, but it is thought to be endangered in some locations. This could be due to changes in the climate affecting the waters in which it lives, pollution or being hunted. There is much more to learn about this incredible species.

Diet

The mosaic crabs' diet is full of a variety of meals. Most notably, they eat a poisonous sea cucumber which they are immune to, as well as fish, sea worms, barnacles, marine plants and more.

Location/Habitat

The mosaic crab resides within the Indo-Pacific region, including in Australian waters and around islands such as Singapore.

Like many other species of crab, the mosaic crab prefers a rocky reef environment and can be found at depths of around 0–5 metres.

Fun Facts

- Can you see a similarity in colouring between this crab and the geography cone snail on page 54? Both creatures warn that they should not be messed with through their striking colours and patterns. This is called aposematism.
- The deadly poison that these crabs inflict is considered a grade one chemical weapon in accordance with the UN Chemical Weapons Convention.
- Their scientific name, *pictor*, actually translates to 'painter' in Latin.
- When these crabs are kept in captivity and unable to eat the poisonous cucumbers, they will slowly lose their toxicity, in some cases completely losing it after 1 month.
- Their toxins are known as saxitoxin and are 1000 times more deadly than cyanide.

Lophozozymus pictor

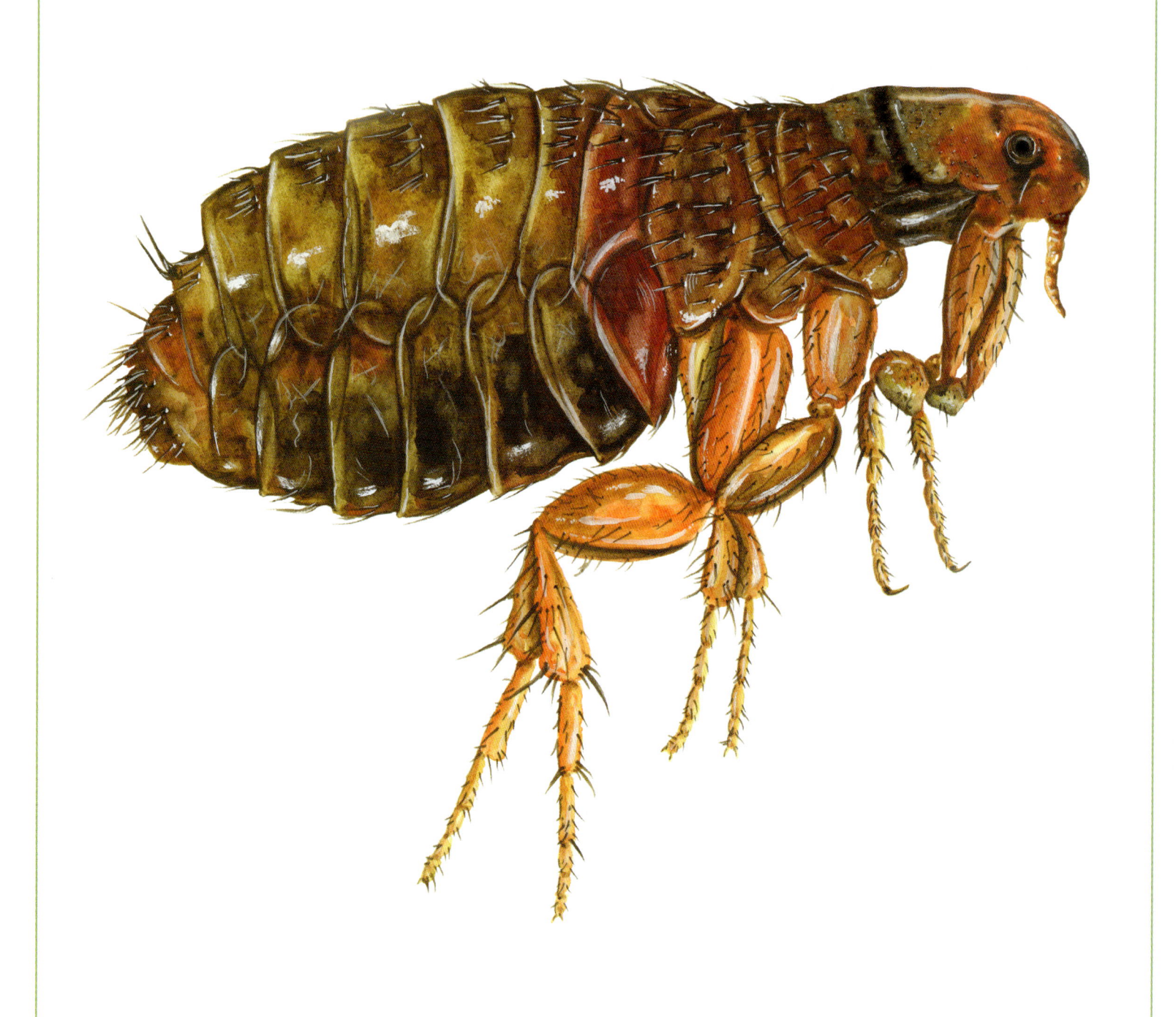

Xenopsylla cheopis

Oriental Rat Flea

Xenopsylla cheopis
(zen-o-sill-a chee-o-pee)

Description

Dark reddish brown in colour, wingless and covered in short hairs, the oriental rat flea has evolved to blend in with the fur of their hosts. These tiny insects reach just 1.5–4 millimetres in length and also feature three pairs of legs. The hind legs are long and powerful and allow for impressive leaps from victim to victim, including distances of 30 centimetres.

1.5-4 millimetres

Danger Factor

When an adult oriental rat flea finds their victim (animals and humans), they bite the skin and let a pool of blood form. They inject their saliva, which contains special chemicals that prevent blood from coagulating, into the wound. This ensures that the blood will flow continuously. These parasitic fleas spread bacteria and after feeding on an infected rat they might then bite a human, transferring the deadly bacteria. This is what happened in the 14th century when the infamous bubonic plague, commonly called the Black Death, took over Asia and Europe, killing approximately 50 million people. Some symptoms of the bubonic plague were fever, and swollen and sore lymph nodes. If untreated, the build-up of dead blood cells in these swollen nodes (known as 'buboes') would lead to death. However, if popped, the contents of the wound could infect the victim's blood, causing them to die from toxic shock. Whilst treating the sick, doctors wore an elaborate mask to protect themselves and help with the terrible smell.

Conservation Status

NOT EVALUATED

Due to the parasitic nature of the oriental rat flea, it is seen as a pest and not one to be concerned about in terms of conservation. Its status has not been evaluated.

Diet

Only attaching themselves to the hosts during feeding, the oriental rat flea can be found feasting on a variety of mammals and birds, including rats, dogs and gerbils. They consume purely blood for their short lives.

Location/Habitat

Found worldwide, the oriental rat flea lives in warm climates in its hosts' nests. This also means that human beds, lounges and clothes are very suitable. They prefer heavily populated areas because human habitats attract rats.

Fun Facts

- There are approximately 10 species of flea that can transmit the plague, along with 2 species of bedbug.
- Unfavourable temperatures, like colder climates, can cause flea pupae to not hatch from their cocoons for up to a year.
- Fleas have very powerful legs, allowing them to jump up to 200 times their body length. Unfortunately for them, they cannot control the direction of their leaps.

Ostrich

Struthio camelus
(struth-e-o camel-us)

Description

The ostrich is a bird, but a flightless one. During its evolution process it has lost the need to fly and use its wings, instead adapting to a new way of living. Because of this, it belongs to a scientific group called ratites, which include the emu, kiwi, rhea and cassowary.

Danger Factor

Around 2.4 metres tall, ostriches have long, powerful legs which help them reach speeds of 70 kilometres per hour. It is these legs, paired with the males' aggressive territorial behaviour, that make them so dangerous. During breeding season, males become extremely dominant and frequently fight one another; they will also fight predators during this time to protect their eggs.

They have an immense store of power behind their legs, each foot has 2 toes, the larger of which has 1 long, sharp claw. This claw is 10 centimetres long and capable of slicing open (and killing) lions, cheetahs, leopards and even humans.

Conservation Status

LEAST CONCERN

The ostrich has a large range and population and so there is currently no cause for concern in terms of their conservation. Even so, they do face risks like habitat destruction and being hunted for their feathers and skin. In fact, a subspecies from the Middle East became extinct in 1992, a warning sign of what might be in store for all species of ostrich if we do not take care.

Diet

Ostriches eat a varied diet. They are primarily herbivores but have been known to feed on insects and even carcasses left by other animals. They are usually quite picky eaters, choosing to take particular seeds from flowers and grass heads. They must eat approximately 3.5 kilograms of food per day to meet their energy needs.

Location/Habitat

This large bird lives throughout many regions of Africa, including Ethiopia, Kenya, Sudan and Zimbabwe. They inhabit savanna climates that are dry or sandy. In the past, however, their range extended to the Arabian Peninsula and south-western Asia before they were hunted to extinction in those places.

Fun Facts

- Their eyes are actually bigger than their brains.
- Both males and females care for eggs. The females watch over them during the day and the males keep guard throughout the night.
- Incredibly, ostriches can live for 50 years!
- You might have heard that ostriches bury their heads in the sand. This is actually a myth, most likely originating from the fact that they have been seen laying down with their heads pressed down flat to the ground. This unusual act is a defence mechanism, ensuring they blend in with their environment and remain hidden from predators.
- One ostrich egg is equivalent to 24 chicken eggs.

Struthio camelus

Taenia solium

Pork Tapeworm

Taenia solium
(tee-nee-uh sole-ee-um)

Description

The pork tapeworm is a parasite that can be found in the small intestines of pigs and potentially transferred to humans through food such as pork. It moves along the gut as it progresses through its life cycle. It is 2.5 metres long, very thin and has numerous hair-like hooks on its head which are used to attach it to the insides of its host.

Danger Factor

What makes the pork tapeworm so dangerous is the fact that it is an intestinal parasite and if it reaches the brain it can cause a very dangerous disease, neurocysticercosis. This can cause eye and muscle damage, seizures and potentially death.

The tapeworm starts in the pig and can be then transferred to a person who eats the infected animal. The effects can be slow and are experienced by both pig and human, and in fact is the leading cause of death related to food-borne disease.

To prevent becoming ill through these creatures, it is important to cook your pork thoroughly, maintain good general health and hygiene or to not consume pork at all.

Conservation Status

NOT EVALUATED

The pork tapeworm's conservation status has not been evaluated, but due to their location, they do not face many threats.

In fact, many researchers are trying to find ways to control their population, including through existing medical treatments.

Diet

Contrary to what you might expect, these worms do not use their head or 'mouthparts' to feed. Instead, they use their bodies to absorb nutrients from the intestinal walls of their host since they do not have a typical digestive system.

Location/Habitat

This species is found across the globe, as they exist wherever pigs live. However, they are more prevalent in regions where uncooked meat is eaten. These locations include Asia, India, Eastern Europe, Latin America and sub-Saharan Africa.

Fun Facts

- Many areas with large Jewish and Muslim populations have low occurrences of this tapeworm, as these populations do not eat pork for cultural reasons.
- These worms can live for 2–3 years.
- The tapeworms that many dogs and cats have are very different to this species. Our pets usually contract their tapeworms from fleas who can carry their larvae.
- It is thought pork tapeworms cause 30% of epilepsy cases in areas where they are endemic.
- They are monoecious. This means that one worm contains both the male and female reproductive systems.

Red-bellied Piranha

Pygocentrus nattereri
(pie-go-cen-trus nat-er-air-ee)

Description

Piranhas have a bad reputation and in popular culture they are often portrayed as aggressive and out to get us. While they are dangerous and can be aggressive, it is not for the reasons that some might believe. In reality, piranhas swarm when the water is low, food is scarce, or they feel threatened.

They grow to around 30 centimetres long and can weigh 3.5 kilograms. Their powerful jaws are packed with razor sharp teeth.

Danger Factor

Because of the piranhas' ability to swarm, their flesh-tearing teeth and their ferocity during feeding, they are considered dangerous. The red-bellied piranha can bite chunks out of the flesh of other river dwellers, and humans will often suffer bites to their hands and feet.

Studies suggest that loud noises, splashing about and emptying fish contents into the water you are swimming in are some key factors linked to piranha attacks. It is thought that in most cases of reported deaths the victim was already dead when the fish decided to snack. Piranhas do not attack those that simply enter the water. However, they can cause serious damage under certain circumstances and should be treated with respect and caution.

Conservation Status

NOT EVALUATED

The red-bellied piranha's conservation status has not yet been evaluated. It has been introduced to a range of new locations over the years, most likely by accident, and is usually killed by government agencies.

Diet

A common misconception is that piranhas only feed by swarming on large mammals. They actually rely on a range of food sources including aquatic invertebrates, insects, fish and even plants. Some piranha species are even totally herbivorous!

Location/Habitat

Found in South America, the red-bellied piranha resides in lakes and rivers in the Amazon and Parana-Paraguay basins, as well as parts of northeast Brazil.

Fun Facts

- Former United States President Theodore Roosevelt came across the piranha in 1913 while travelling around South America. In his book, *Through the Brazilian Wilderness*, he wrote: 'They will devour alive any wounded man or beast; for blood in the water excites them to madness.' This comment is one reason why piranhas got such a bad reputation.
- Part of their mating display includes swimming around in circles.
- Piranhas can smell a single drop of blood in 200 litres of water.
- When going after its prey, the piranha will go for the eyes and tail, in order to ensure that the victim cannot get away.

Pygocentrus nattereri

Missulena occatoria

Red-headed Mouse Spider

Missulena occatoria
(miss-you-lee-na oc-ca-tor-ia)

Description

In this species, females are approximately twice the size of males, reaching 35 millimetres to the males' 15. This is not uncommon for spiders. While the males might be smaller, they are definitely more striking! Females of this species are dark brown or black in colour, while the males have a striking red head and jaws and a royal blue or black abdomen.

Danger Factor

Both sexes of the red-headed mouse spider contain a venom toxic enough to kill a human, although this is very uncommon. In most cases, this spider only causes minor injuries. This is because the mouse spider prefers to give dry bites, meaning no venom is injected. This allows it to save its small reserve of venom for future needs.

Conservation Status

NOT EVALUATED

The red-headed mouse spider is a common meal for a variety of creatures, including scorpions, centipedes, bandicoots and even parasitic wasps, which can hijack the spider's nervous system and make it act according to the wasp's needs.

Red-headed mouse spiders are common, though you will only come across them in the early months of the year when the males are outside of their burrows, searching for a female.

Diet

The majority of the red-headed mouse spider's diet consists of insects and other spiders, however they have also been documented eating larger creatures like lizards and frogs.

Location/Habitat

Endemic across mainland Australia, the red-headed mouse spider can be found in areas close to waterways and occasionally garden beds. They live in burrows up to 55 centimetres deep which are lined with sticks, twigs, leaves and a flap of silk at the entrance.

Fun Facts

- There are 8 different species of mouse spider, and the red-headed is thought to be the most toxic.
- After hatching, baby red-headed mouse spiders will use a small carpet of silk to catch the wind and carry them away from the hatch site. This method is known as 'ballooning'.
- It is not entirely clear why they are called 'mouse spiders'. However, it is thought that they were mistaken for mice in the past due to their large size and deep burrows.
- The bite of a red-headed mouse spider is often compared to that of a Sydney funnel-web spider. There have even been cases where funnel-web spider antivenom was successfully used to treat a mouse-spider bite.
- Because they look so different, it took many years after their discovery before the male and female red-headed mouse spiders were recognised as the same species.

Red Devil Squid

Dosidicus gigas
(doe-sid-e-cus gi-gas)

Description

Weighing in at 50 kilograms and around 2 metres long, the red devil squid is the largest of the flying squid family (Ommastrephidae). It has 8 arms and 2 tentacles. The difference between these two types of limb is that arms generally have suckers all the way down and tentacles only have suckers at the tip.

Danger Factor

If you are unlucky enough to be in the water with these squid, you might very well be in danger… Fast, strong and sometimes aggressive, they have been known to attack humans, usually dragging them down into the water and ripping into them with their tentacles and beak. But there is no need to worry, they are generally more curious than anything and it is unlikely for humans to be on their menu.

Conservation Status

DATA DEFICIENT

Because they prefer to stay deep in the sea, there is very little known about the population size or conservation status of the red devil squid.

There are, however, a few species known to prey on them. These include sperm whales, striped marlin and even deep-sea sharks.

Diet

The red devil squid has hundreds of suckers located on their arms. These seemingly unimportant features are actually wonderful adaptations that assist in mating and also capturing and holding on to their prey while they use their sharp beak-like mouths to eat.

These squid like to eat crustaceans and deep-sea fish such as lanternfish. Occasionally, they even resort to cannibalism.

Location/Habitat

This species lives in the eastern Pacific Ocean, from northern California to southern Chile, and can be found from depths just beneath the surface to 1000 metres down.

Fun Facts

- They also go by the name 'Humboldt squid' and 'jumbo flying squid'.
- These squid have evolved the ability to decrease their oxygen requirements in order to survive in deep, low-oxygen waters.
- They can change their colouring to blend in with their environment, as well as to give a warning before attacking. Their name 'red devil' was given to them because of their vibrant red colour.
- They move by jet propulsion, sucking water into their mantle (the top section of their bodies) and quickly expelling it through their siphon (a tube exiting the body).
- They only live for approximately 1–2 years.

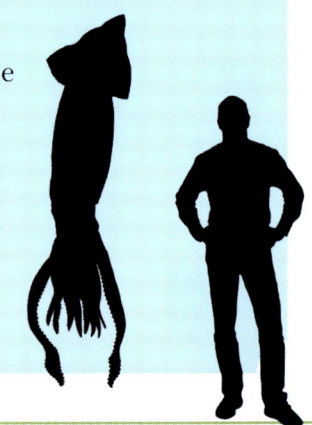

Dosidicus gigas

Macropus rufus

Red Kangaroo

Macropus rufus
(macro-pus ru-fuss)

Description

The red kangaroo is the largest marsupial in the world, reaching up to 1.8 metres tall and weighing 90 kilograms. Their size makes them the most dangerous kangaroo species.

They gain their name from their warm red and brown fur that helps them to blend in with their environment. But some found more easterly can be blue or grey in colour.

Danger Factor

Kangaroos in general are known for 'boxing'. This is when they fight by hitting out with their forepaws and kicking with their large, strong feet, while using their tail as a support. The stronger kicks of a red kangaroo have the potential to disembowel a victim.

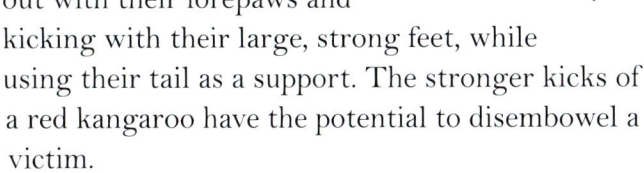

The majority of fights among kangaroos occur between males competing with one another for dominance and mating rights. Kangaroos have also been recorded injuring humans who stray into their territory, scratching and pushing with their powerful claws.

Conservation Status

LEAST CONCERN

Dingoes and wild dogs usually prey on joeys, and can occasionally kill adult kangaroos.

However, due to the large number of red kangaroos distributed throughout Australia, they are of least concern in terms of conservation. They are even considered a pest by farmers whose crops they consume.

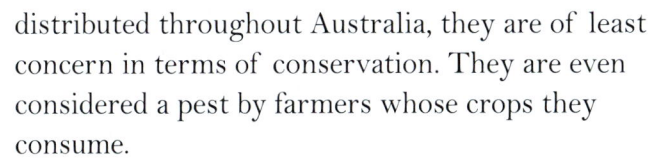

Nonetheless, it is important we look after them as they have an important role in managing vegetation in their environment.

Diet

As red kangaroos are herbivores, they rely on grasses and other plants for nutrients and struggle during drought. They have even been recorded to travel over 200 kilometres in order to find grasslands that have had rainfall.

Location/Habitat

Endemic to Australia, the red kangaroo is found in dry and arid zones, primarily in the centre of the country. Their preferred habitats are deserts, grasslands, scrublands and shrublands.

Fun Facts

- With their strong legs and tail, the red kangaroo can leap distances of 8 metres and heights of 3 metres.
- They have been recorded to live up to 22 years in the wild, and 30 years in captivity!
- When born, the joey is just a tiny 2.5 centimetres long.
- It is quite common for a mother kangaroo to raise multiple young at the same time. These babies are usually at different stages of life: one suckling, another in the pouch and one weaned outside the pouch.

Red Lionfish

Pterois volitans
(tero-is voli-tans)

Description

Growing to 38 centimetres long and covered in white and red-brown stripes, the red lionfish gains its name from its similarities to a lion. The reddish brown fins and spines framing its face can be compared to the striking mane of a lion.

Danger Factor

Much like the reef stonefish on page 105, the red lionfish has 13 venomous spines along its dorsal fins. These painful evolutionary adaptations are the reason this striking fish is so dangerous. A sting from these spines can cause terrible pain, nausea, seizures, paralysis of limbs and even heart failure in some cases. It is estimated that there are up to 50,000 stings across the globe each year.

Conservation Status

NOT EVALUATED

As you can imagine, any species of fish that has so many toxic spines will have a limited number of predators, and this is the case for the red lionfish. They are considered invasive in many regions and are known to drive away important native species that are vital to coral reefs.

Even so, these beautiful animals do face some threats due to ocean pollution and its impact on their food sources.

Diet

The red lionfish usually feasts on small fish, shrimp and crayfish. It has also been documented engaging in cannibalism occasionally.

Location/Habitat

These fish can be found living along much of the coast of Australia and throughout the Indo-Pacific region, including Malaysia, southern Korea and southern Japan.

They spend their days concealed in nooks and crannies and come out to swim in coral reefs at night.

Fun Facts

- They are also known as 'fire fish'.
- Instead of swimming away when scared, the red lionfish will stand its ground and point its spines toward the threat.
- Their vibrant colouring is used to warn off potential predators, letting them know that they are venomous.
- It is thought that the antivenom used for the red lionfish will also work for the reef stonefish, found on page 105.
- Even though these fish are very dangerous, they are still often sold as pets.

Pterois volitans

Synanceia verrucosa

Reef Stonefish

Synanceia verrucosa
(sigh-nan-sea-a ver-ru-co-sa)

Description

As its name suggests, this 30-centimetre long fish looks just like a stone or maybe a growth-covered piece of coral. It blends perfectly with its environment and this is one reason that it is so dangerous.

Danger Factor

It has numerous venom-filled spines on its dorsal fins, which it uses against oncoming threats. A prick from one of these spines can cause excruciating pain, breathing issues, heart failure and possible death. In order to protect yourself from this fish, it is important to stay alert and wear suitable reef shoes when wading through their habitats.

Conservation Status

LEAST CONCERN

Fortunately, the reef stonefish is not preyed on by many creatures. Its harsh features and preference for living in protected nooks and crannies mean that it faces very few threats and is considered of least concern within the conservation world.

Diet

Although they are slow-moving creatures for most of their lives, these fish can be incredibly fast when it comes to feeding and save their energy for short-burst surprise attacks. They stay hidden while waiting for a fish, shrimp or crab to swim past. When this happens, they launch out and snatch them up lightning fast.

Location/Habitat

The reef stonefish is found around coral reefs and buried in sand in the Indo-West Pacific at around 20 metres deep. They live in waters around Japan, Sri Lanka and the coast of Africa and in the Red and South China Seas. They can even be found along the coasts of Australia, including the Great Barrier Reef.

Fun Facts
- In rare cases, the reef stonefish has been sold in fish markets for its meat.
- Certain species of ray and shark are some of the very few sea creatures that prey on the reef stonefish.
- It is considered the most venomous fish in the world.

Rough-skinned Newt

Taricha granulosa
(tar-e-ka gran-you-low-sa)

Description

Newts are a type of salamander and these semi-aquatic amphibians usually look like a blend of a frog and a lizard. The skin on the back of these newts is coarse and grainy, which is how they got their name. This skin is also covered in toxin.

Danger Factor

Although relatively small, 15 centimetres on average, these peculiar creatures can cause skin irritation in humans when picked up and, if eaten, paralysis. The rough-skinned newt will lay on rocks with its brown back on show, and when under threat it will warn off predators by bending its head and tail upwards and displaying its vibrant orange stomach. It is the creatures that do not heed this warning and eat the newt that end up with the deadly toxins in their stomachs.

Conservation Status

LEAST CONCERN

This unusual amphibian lives in a variety of locations and is plentiful. Estimates suggest that there are over 100,000 individuals, meaning it is fortunately of least concern in terms of conservation.

Even so, it is important to drive cautiously when near their habitats.

Diet

Whether in water or on land, the rough-skinned newt can be found snacking on insects, snails, amphibians like frogs or other newts, as well as other aquatic invertebrates.

Location/Habitat

The rough-skinned newt can be found around the Pacific coast of North America, including places like Alaska, California and Santa Cruz county.

Like many other species of amphibian, this newt spends its days in woodlands and valleys, residing around rocks and logs as well as in lakes and ponds.

Fun Facts

- Amazingly, a species of snake called the common garter snake is resistant to their deadly toxins. It is one of very few predators which the newt faces.
- Groups of rough-skinned newts have been found in water as deep as 12 metres.
- During the breeding season, males change their appearance and become smoother and lighter. Parts of their toes and tail also become more noticeable.
- Females lay their eggs onto decaying organic matter so that the young can consume it as they develop. They also cover these eggs with toxins to make sure predators steer clear.
- It is estimated that these newts can live up to 18 years of age!

Taricha granulosa

Isurus oxyrinchus

Shortfin Mako Shark

Isurus oxyrinchus
(is-ur-us oxy-rin-cuss)

Description

Averaging 3–4 metres long and weighing 60–135 kilograms, these sharks have long, streamlined bodies and thick, strong tail fins which help them pick up speed quickly. They can even reach speeds of 80 kilometres per hour for a short burst, or 56 kilometres per hour for more sustained swimming. This makes them the fastest shark in the world.

Danger Factor

Most shark attacks happen within the water, but the shortfin mako shark has a record of being just as dangerous outside its habitat. When reeled into fishing boats after being captured, they often thrash around to try to free themselves, sometimes biting or crushing anyone unlucky enough to get in their way. It is their slender, powerful bodies, sharp teeth and violent movements when threatened that make them incredibly dangerous outside of the water and sets them apart from other sharks. Although they have only killed a few people since the 1970s, they are still considered especially dangerous because of the injuries they can cause.

Conservation Status

ENDANGERED

These sharks are commonly caught for their meat, fins, liver and oil, which is sought after because of its high quality. They are also popular among big-game recreational fishers. Although they are released back in most cases, some sharks will die not long after because of injuries sustained or the stress of being caught. These factors have led to their decline in a variety of locations.

Diet

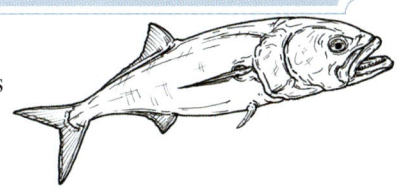

Bluefish make up the majority of this shark's diet, but they will also eat other sea creatures such as other fish, octopuses, squid, dolphins and turtles.

Location/Habitat

Typically found at depths of at least 150 metres, the shortfin mako shark lives in both temperate and tropical oceans across the globe, including the Indian, Pacific and Atlantic Oceans, as well as the Mediterranean and Red Seas.

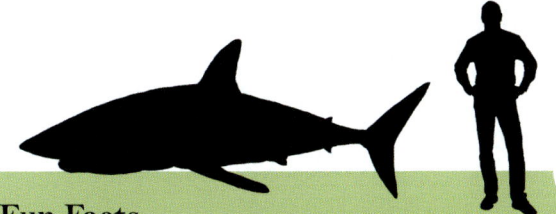

Fun Facts

- They sometimes swim for thousands of kilometres in just one month in order to hunt for prey or find a suitable mate.
- They have been recorded to live as long as 32 years.
- They play a vital role in population control within their ecosystems, even switching to prey on a different species when they notice a decline in population of the fish they were initially preying on.
- Swimming at such fast speeds, they are able to leap out of the water, and up to 9 metres into the air!

Six-spot Burnet Moth

Zygaena filipendulae
(zig-aye-nah fil-ee-pen-dew-lay)

Description

Like its name suggests, the six-spot burnet moth features six vibrant red spots on its dark, charcoal-coloured wings, which are approximately 3–4 centimetres across when open.

Danger Factor

Although these moths look very unalarming, they are indeed dangerous. When feeling threatened, they release hydrogen cyanide which they obtained from the plants they ate while in the caterpillar stage. This cautions predators that they are poisonous and should not be messed with. They can be lethal to small birds and lizards.

Conservation Status

NOT EVALUATED

Although the conservation status of the six-spot burnet moth is yet to be confirmed, it is thought that their numbers are high, and they are not in any danger of extinction.

However, like many species which rely on grasslands and habitats near civilisation, their range is being severely reduced or destroyed by human intervention.

Diet

Attracted to a range of plants such as thistles, knapweeds and wildflowers, this gentle and unhurried moth spends its days fluttering about and feeding on nectar. As caterpillars, they consume a plant called bird's-foot trefoil.

Location/Habitat

These small moths are the most widely spread species of burnet moth in the United Kingdom. In order to see one, you must travel to England, Ireland, Wales or Scotland around June to August. They enjoy sand dunes, cliff edges, grassland and woodland habitats.

Fun Facts

- There are other species of burnet moths that feature wings with 5 spots.
- In their caterpillar phase, six-spot burnet moths are actually a vibrant yellow and black, another colour scheme to ward off predators.
- Before the caterpillars turn into moths, they feast and then hibernate for a few months.
- They have evolved to mimic the black and red colours of the cinnabar, another species of moth which is infamous for poisoning horses.
- The six-spot burnet moth is found in large groups, typically reaching around several hundred individuals.

Zygaena filipendulae

Hapalochlaena maculosa

Southern Blue-ringed Octopus

Hapalochlaena maculosa
(hap-al-o-clay-na mack-you-low-sa)

Description

The southern blue-ringed octopus is nocturnal, meaning it is active during the night and sleeps or hides during the day, making it quite tricky to spot. When you do get a chance to see them, they are just 20 centimetres long and weigh 26 grams.

Danger Factor

Despite their small size, they can cause a lot of harm! Their electric blue rings glow brightly when they are threatened and act as a warning to predators. The danger is not in simply touching a blue-ringed octopus, but in being bitten by one. They have a small beak-like mouth hidden under their body and this is what does the damage. When bitten, powerful tetrodotoxins from the octopus's saliva enter the body. These are the same toxins as found in the tiger pufferfish (on page 118). A victim may not even know they have been bitten until they start feeling dizzy a few minutes later. After this, they will develop trouble breathing and then muscle paralysis. If the toxins do not wear off after 24 hours, the victim will likely die.

Conservation Status

LEAST CONCERN

Blue-ringed octopuses are found over a wide area and have a large enough population that they are considered of least concern. However, they do face a few threats. One of these is being captured for the pet or aquarium trades. Another is global warming, which is destroying their habitats.

Diet

They enjoy feasting at night on fish or crustaceans, including crabs, shellfish and shrimp. These octopuses have a number of techniques to catch their prey. One is to bite the victim and inject their venom into it, killing it instantly. Another is to release a cloud of venom into the water around the prey. The venom seeps into their victim's gills and paralyses them.

Location/Habitat

As their name suggests, the southern blue-ringed octopus is found off the southern coasts of Australia, all the way from eastern Victoria to south-western Australia and Tasmania.

They live at relatively shallow depths of up to 20 metres, most often in and around rockpools, reefs and seagrass.

Fun Facts

- When they are not feeling threatened, these octopuses are a bland creamy yellow or brown shade and can be easily overlooked.
- Like many species of octopus, the female guards her eggs for several months after laying them, all the while not eating or leaving her nest. Soon after they hatch and her mission is complete, she will die.
- It is thought that there could be 4 different species of blue-ringed octopus!
- The deadly toxins are also found in octopus eggs, most likely as an extra precaution to deter predators from feasting on the young.

Spider-tailed Horned Viper

Pseudocerastes urarachnoides
(sew-dos-er-aystes your-a-rack-noides)

Description

The spider-tailed horned viper was not officially recorded as a new species until 2006. Previous to this, many people thought the rare snake was just a viper with a deformed tail. We now know that it has raised, dappled brown scales that assist it with blending into its rocky environment and an impressive tail unlike any other snake.

Danger Factor

That is not a mutated spider on this viper's tail, but rather an evolutionary adaptation which acts as a fleshy lure for nearby prey. The snake uses it to mimic the movements of a spider, wiggling it about and moving the individual elongated scales which look awfully similar to spider legs. When a bird comes close to peck at the 'spider', the viper springs out and catches its lunch. This ability to imitate a different species gives these snakes a new level of danger. Its prey-catching method does not come without risk. If the viper is not quick enough, the bird could bite off its lure!

Conservation Status

DATA DEFICIENT

Since this species was first described very recently, there is little known about its population size or conservation status. However, it is expected that it faces similar threats to many other species of viper, for example poaching for the exotic pet trade, occasional killing by locals and habitat destruction.

Diet

Using its magnificent tail adaptation, this viper attracts birds and occasionally lizards to prey on. Interestingly, it is less common for local species of bird to be tricked by its lure, suggesting that they are on to the false snack.

Location/Habitat

The spider-tailed horned viper lives in the Zagros Mountains of western Iran. It is very difficult to spot because it is a similar colour to the rocks where it lives. Further, it likes to hide in cracks and crevasses, leaving just its spider-like tail exposed to potential prey.

Fun Facts

- It also goes by the name 'false horned viper'.
- The collective noun for a group of vipers is a 'generation'.
- They are not born with their lures but rather develop them over the course of their lives.
- The pupils of vipers are slit shaped in order to better assist them in seeing their prey before ambushing them.

Pseudocerastes urarachnoides

Sarcophilus harrisii

Tasmanian Devil

Sarcophilus harrisii
(sar-coff-ilus harris-ee-eye)

Description

The white markings on Tasmanian devils' chests and spots on their rump assist them in the night with locating the front and back of one another, often for males wanting to fight. Although they are small, reaching just 60 centimetres and weighing 12 kilograms, they have enough strength in their jaws to crush bone.

Danger Factor

Tasmanian devils are apex predators, packed full of muscle, power, sharp teeth and strong jaws, which they often use wrestling and biting each other. They will also inflict these inbuilt weapons on those that pose a threat, including humans and any animal not fast enough to flee. Although they do not attack humans often, and in fact would rather avoid us altogether, they will certainly do some damage if they feel threatened. For humans, injuries include severe bites and scratches which can lead to infection but for other animals, it is a lot more sinister. There is no mistaking their ferocity when you hear the wild noises they make when feeding or catch sight of their enormous mouths open and packed with strong teeth.

Conservation Status

ENDANGERED

Unfortunately, the Tasmanian devil suffers a terrible and destructive disease called devil facial tumour disease. This is thought to be transmitted by the devils biting one another, which they do very often during mating season.

This devastating illness, paired with the fact that they are being hit by cars and occasionally killed by farmers who consider them pests, means the Tasmanian devil population has fallen drastically. Since 1996, 90% have disappeared.

Diet

These marsupials are carnivorous but will more often than not feed on carrion (already dead animals) instead of hunting for themselves. Their diet is made up of insects, birds, wallabies and even cattle.

Location/Habitat

Unsurprisingly, the Tasmanian devil lives in Tasmania, Australia. However, you might not expect that it was once found across mainland Australia. They disappeared from the mainland around 4000 years ago, most likely because they were unable to compete with the arrival of the dingo from south Asia.

In Tasmania, these animals are the top predator and can be found living in a variety of habitats, including woodlands, open forests and heathlands.

Fun Facts
- Their scientific name actually means 'meat lover'!
- Devils have been recorded to travel for up to 16 kilometres a day for food, using their keen sense of smell to help them find stinky carrion.
- Their common name, 'devil', was given to them after early settlers heard their terrifying sounds and saw their black fur and red ears.

Tiger Pufferfish

Takifugu rubripes
(tacky-foo-goo rube-ripes)

Description

Despite their name and appearance, the tiger pufferfish is not always so bloated. When deflated, they look like a regular fish but when a predator approaches to eat them or they are looking to defend themselves, they will quickly pump water into their stomachs and fill up like a balloon.

Danger Factor

The tiger pufferfish contains tetrodotoxin in its body which can cause paralysis and respiratory failure to those animals and humans that consume it. Although this fish is extremely dangerous, it is also considered a delicacy, called 'fugu', and can sell for hundreds of dollars per kilogram. If chefs are not careful to slice away all the dangerous parts, it can be disastrous. In fact, this pufferfish was the cause of nearly 50 deaths between 1983 and 1992. With more awareness and tougher regulations around preparing fugu, that number has dropped massively.

Conservation Status

NEAR THREATENED

Up to 10,000 tonnes of fugu is eaten each year, so you can imagine how many of these ocean dwellers are being killed to meet that demand.

Unfortunately, due to the high demand for tiger pufferfish their numbers are falling. They are being caught through a highly effective fishing method called long-line fishing, and this is contributing to their over-capture.

Diet

These fish mainly eat molluscs, worms and clams, using their powerful beaks to crack open the shells.

Amazingly, the pufferfish is thought to get their toxins from the foods they eat. Many of the animals they consume have toxin-containing bacteria inside them and the pufferfish is able to store this inside their own bodies.

Location/Habitat

Found in parts of the north-western Pacific Ocean, such as the East China and Yellow Seas as well as the Sea of Japan, the tiger pufferfish spends its time at depths of around 10–150 metres.

Fun Facts

→ Mentioned in *The Illustrated Encyclopaedia of Ugly Animals*, the ocean sunfish is actually a close relative of the pufferfish.

→ The same toxins can also be found in the blue-ringed octopus.

→ Not only are tiger pufferfish eaten, they are also used in Chinese medicines.

→ Cases of pufferfish poisoning have been recorded all the way back to ancient Egyptian times!

Takifugu rubripes

Balistoides viridescens

Titan Triggerfish

Balistoides viridescens
(bal-is-toy-ds vir-e-des-ens)

Description

Reaching on average 40–60 centimetres long, some titan triggerfish have even been documented at 75 centimetres! Given their size, it is no surprise that this fish is incredibly powerful and not one to be messed with.

Danger Factor

Titan triggerfish have caused injuries varying from tears in a diver's gear, bumps and bruises to more serious damage like divers being knocked out or having their ears bitten off. These injuries are inflected only to protect the fish's young. Which, when you think about it, just makes titan triggerfish wonderful parents! These fish can also be dangerous if eaten because they are often infected with a toxin called ciguatoxin which they absorb through eating marine algae. Although harmless to the triggerfish, it can be fatal to humans who consume it.

Conservation Status

NOT EVALUATED

The conservation status of the titan triggerfish has not yet been evaluated. However, because of their interesting evolutionary adaptations, they do not face many natural threats or predators.

Diet

Titan triggerfish have evolved strong jaws with powerful teeth and are equipped to crush and consume the tough shells of any prey they eat. These meals generally consist of hard-shelled invertebrates such as sea urchins and crabs, as well as the algae mentioned above.

Location/Habitat

The titan triggerfish lives deep in the central Pacific and Indian Oceans, including locations around Australia, Thailand, Indonesia and Fiji. They are usually found at depths of 10–30 metres, feeding during the day and sleeping at night.

They live in heavily monitored territories that extend vertically rather than horizontally, in a cone shape. This means if you accidentally enter their territory, the best way to escape is not to swim up, but to swim across.

Fun Facts

- Males often charge after anything that encroaches onto their territory while they are guarding their nest or during breeding season.
- Each eye can move independently!
- They are called 'triggerfish' because they can lock their larger dorsal fin in place by erecting a smaller second fin. The large fin can only be unlocked by depressing the second, 'trigger' fin. Triggerfish raise their fins as a protection against predators and to anchor them in place when they are in rocks or crevices.
- They also go by the name 'moustache triggerfish', because of the dark shade above their mouth.
- This is the largest species in the triggerfish family.

Vampire Bat

Desmodus rotundus
(des-mo-dus ro-tun-dus)

Description

The vampire bat is small and brown, with pointed ears and an upturned nose known as 'leaf nosed'. It has evolved large eyes to help it see in the dark and a great sense of smell to help it find prey.

Danger Factor

At approximately 8 centimetres long, this small mammal goes unnoticed when out stalking its dinner. It will usually fly to a place near its victim and then creep over to them, staying quiet so as not to wake or startle them. The bat then makes a tiny slice in the skin from which it licks up the victim's blood. Infection from the wound can occur in both animal and human victims and, if left untreated, can be fatal. Despite this, vampire bats are far from the blood-sucking, evil creatures that they are made out to be. In fact, they are very gentle creatures just needing a meal.

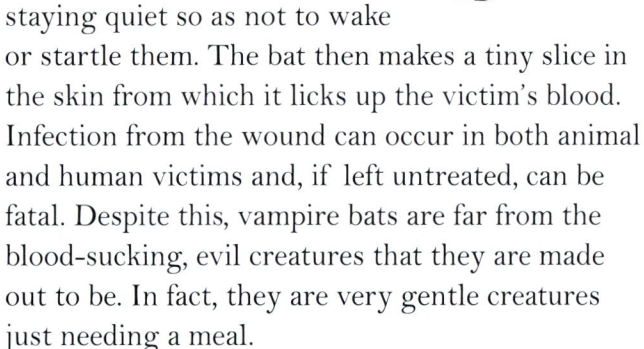

Conservation Status

LEAST CONCERN

The vampire bat is skilled at adapting to its surroundings, so any changes to its habitat do not affect it as much as those same changes might affect other animals. These bats also have a wide range and high population which means they are of least concern in terms of conservation.

They are often seen as a nuisance because they are thought to carry rabies and are considered a parasite. However, we must respect how important these bats are to the ecosystem and make sure they are cared for.

Diet

This species has evolved over time to feed on blood. They have developed large, sharp teeth and grooves on their tongue which help them consume it.

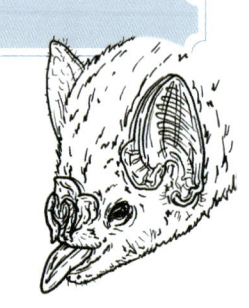

They feed on farm animals, snakes, crocodiles and even humans.

Location/Habitat

The vampire bat is found throughout parts of South America, including Bolivia, Uruguay, Paraguay, northern Chile and Argentina. They prefer warmer climates and being in large groups. Anywhere between 20–5000 of these bats can be found living in caves, tree cavities, empty buildings and similar places.

Fun Facts

- If you enter a cave where vampire bats live, you will be overpowered by the strong stench of their droppings. The smell is ammonia and is due to their blood diets.
- They are thought to live for as long as 12 years in the wild.
- For the first month of life, baby vampire bats will drink their mother's milk, then transition to a blood diet.
- Their saliva has anticoagulant properties which allows them to drink as much blood as they need from their victim.

Desmodus rotundus

Gulo gulo

Wolverine

Gulo gulo
(g-youl-o g-youl-o)

Description

Averaging at 95 centimetres long and 13 kilograms in weight, the wolverine is a threatening creature that you would not want to come across in the wild.

Danger Factor

Like the Tasmanian devil on page 117, they have unique markings on their chests and give off quite the ferocious display. However, this is usually exaggerated in order to prove themselves in the face of larger competing predators. Their muscular bodies, powerful teeth and sharp claws enable them to unleash upon animals much larger than they are, so it is good to keep your distance and appreciate these animals from afar.

Conservation Status

LEAST CONCERN

The wolverine's habitat is being affected by the encroachment of houses, roads and businesses. Because they are seen as pests by farmers whose livestock they attack, they are sometimes trapped or poisoned. They are also sometimes killed for their fur. Amazingly, there are documented cases of wolverines turning traps over to set them off and even burying them.

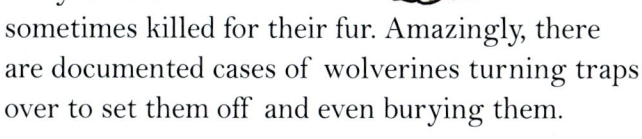

Aside from these factors, their population remains high and their conservation status is of least concern.

Diet

The wolverine has a high kill drive and is known to both scavenge and kill their own prey. They eat a variety of plants and animals such as rabbits, eggs, squirrels and even reindeer. They are known to store their leftovers under the cold snow in order to preserve their food for as long as possible.

Location/Habitat

These creatures are tricky to see because they live in such remote places in the northern regions of Asia, Europe and North America, including Canada, Mongolia and northern China. Their long, dense fur has evolved to help them live in cold woodlands, mountains and other similar habitats.

Fun Facts

- Their scientific name translates to 'glutton', which is apt considering their greediness around food.
- They can live to 13 years old.
- Wolverines have a playful side and have been known to play with objects as though they were toys.
- A baby wolverine is called a 'kit' or 'cub'.
- As you might have already guessed, this wild animal inspired the famous Marvel character, Wolverine.
- They are actually the largest member of the weasel family.

Yellow Fever Mosquito

Aedes aegypti
(ay-e-dees egypt-eye)

Description

To the average person, most mosquitos look the same. It is not until you get up close and personal that you begin to see what makes them unique.

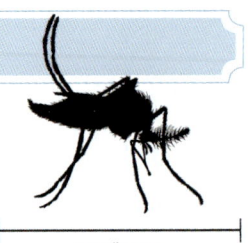

4-7 millimetres

The yellow fever mosquito has unique patterning on its mid-section, also known as a thorax, and ranges from 4–7 millimetres long. As with other mosquito species, the females are larger than the males and have slightly different features.

Danger Factor

Female yellow fever mosquitos use their proboscis to puncture their victim's skin and feed on their blood. This can transfer a virus from one host to another through the mosquito. In fact, there are many viruses transmitted this way, including Zika, dengue, chikungunya and of course yellow fever. According to the World Health Organization, dengue fever is the most critical mosquito-borne viral disease in the world. Symptoms of these viruses include headaches, body aches, vomiting, jaundice, fever and eventually problems with a person's organs. This can lead to liver failure and possible death. It is estimated that there are one million deaths caused by mosquitos every year and the yellow fever mosquito is responsible for most of them.

Conservation Status

A GLOBALLY INVASIVE SPECIES

There are measures in place to eradicate yellow fever mosquitos because the viruses they transmit are destructive to communities around the world. However, all species of mosquito play a role in their environment, for example by pollinating fruits and flowers, or by being a food source for other animals such as bats, frogs and fish.

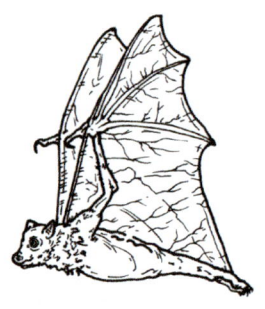

Diet

Females generally survive on the blood they suck from humans and other animals, preferring to feed on mammals. Males feed purely on nectar found in plants.

Location/Habitat

The yellow fever mosquito comes from Africa. It is thought to have spread across the world via ships travelling to unaffected areas many years ago.

It can now be found across 47 countries including Brazil, Colombia and Mexico.

Fun Facts

- Another term for dengue is the 'break-bone fever', due to the intense pain victims feel.
- It is thought that more American troops died from yellow fever during the Spanish-American War than from enemy fire.
- Ever wondered why it is called yellow fever? It is because one of the symptoms of this virus is jaundice, a condition that causes the skin and eyes to turn yellow.
- These mosquitos live for up to a month.
- A Nobel Prize was given to Max Theiler in 1951 for creating a vaccine against yellow fever. This is the only time a Nobel Prize has been given for creating a vaccine.

Aedes aegypti

About the author

Sami Bayly is a natural history illustrator based in Newcastle, Australia, who loves all things weird and wonderful. She finds the beauty in all animals regardless of their appearance or reputation, and hopes to share her appreciation with others.

Sami's first book, *The Illustrated Encyclopaedia of Ugly Animals*, won the Children's Indie Book of the Year Award and has been shortlisted for the CBCA Eve Pownall Award, the ABIA Book of the Year for Younger Children, the Australian Book Design Awards, and longlisted for the ABA Booksellers' Choice 2020 Book of the Year Awards.

To keep up to date you can follow Sami on Instagram
@samibayly

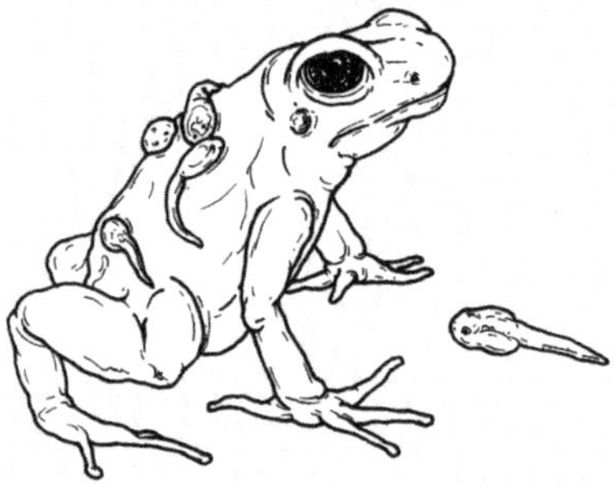
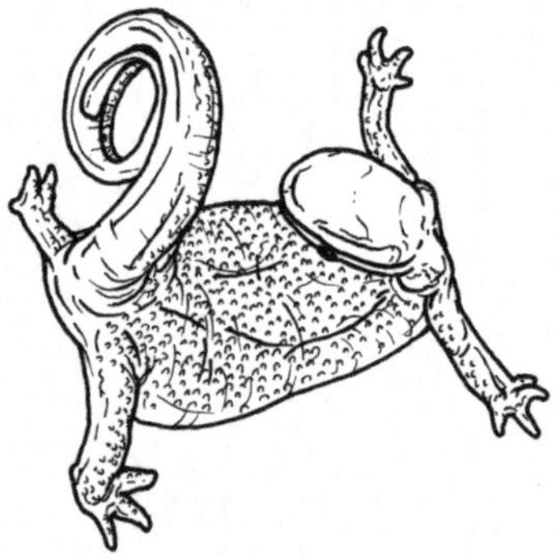
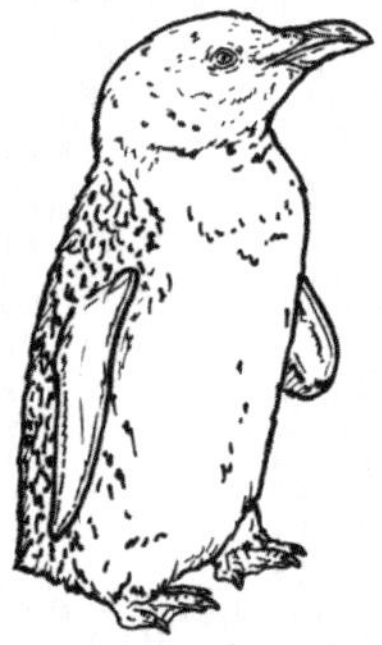
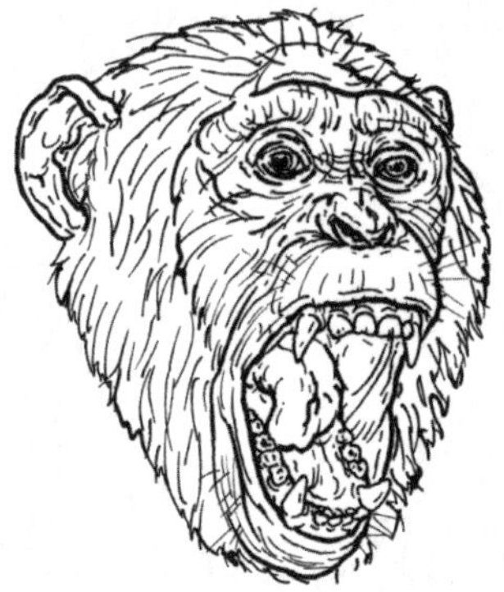
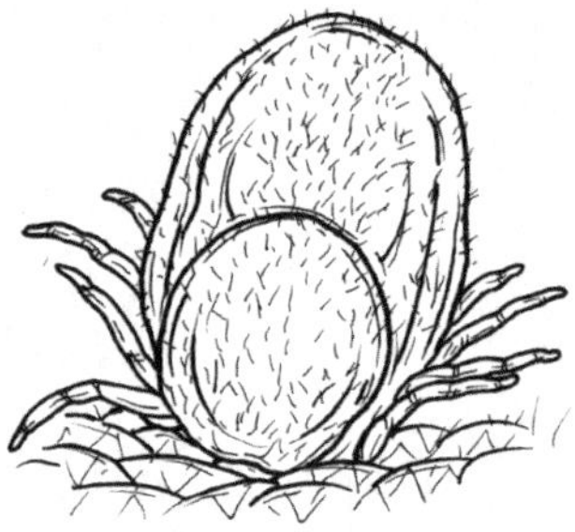
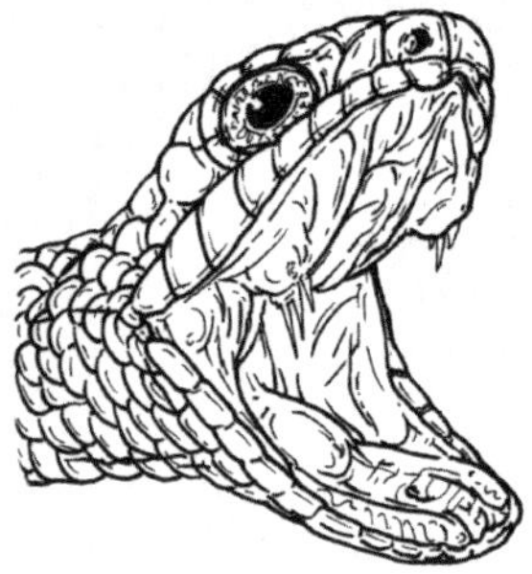
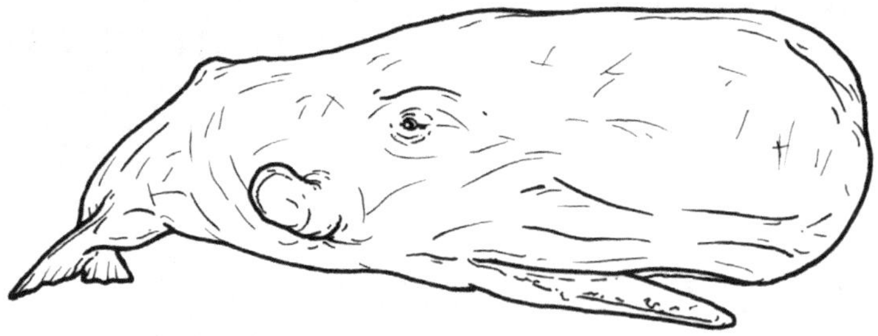
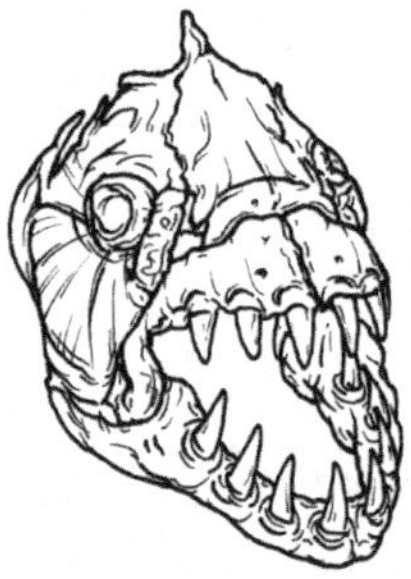
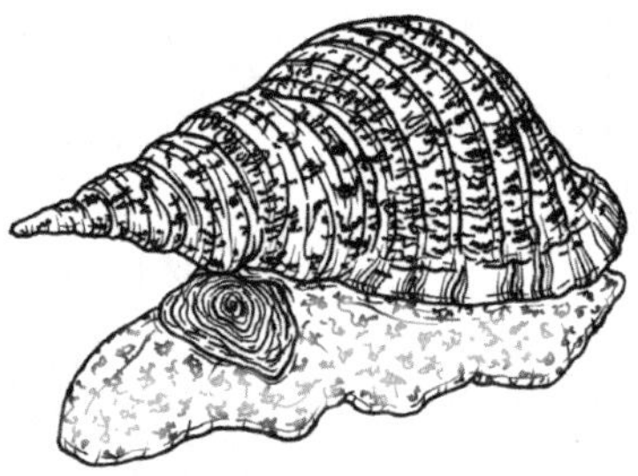
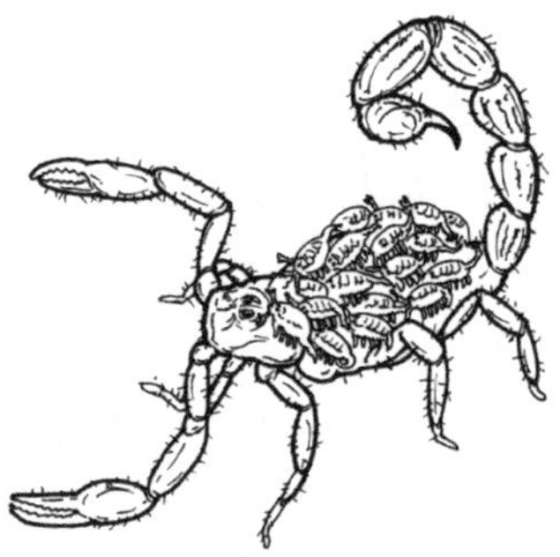
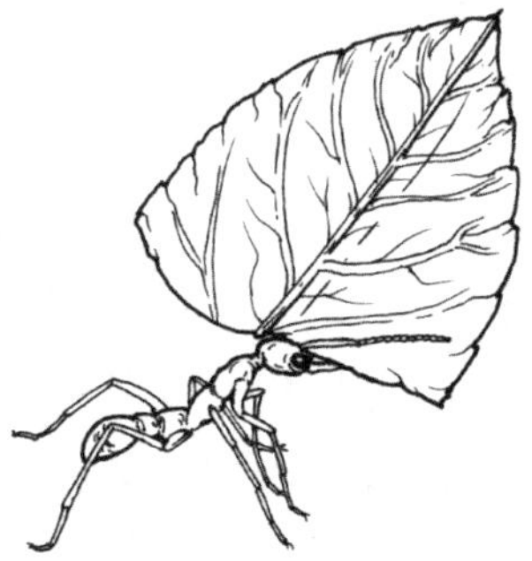
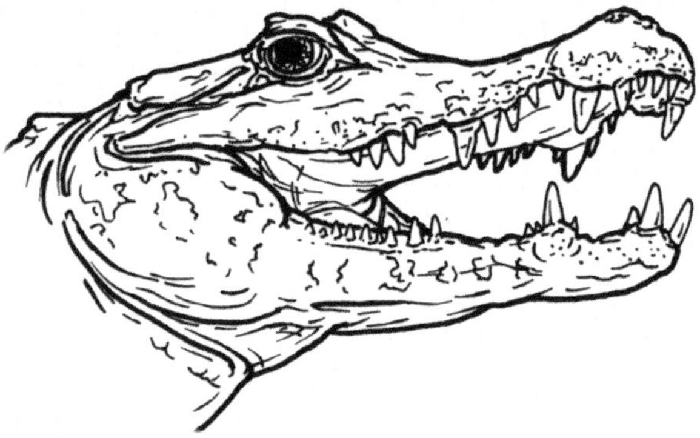
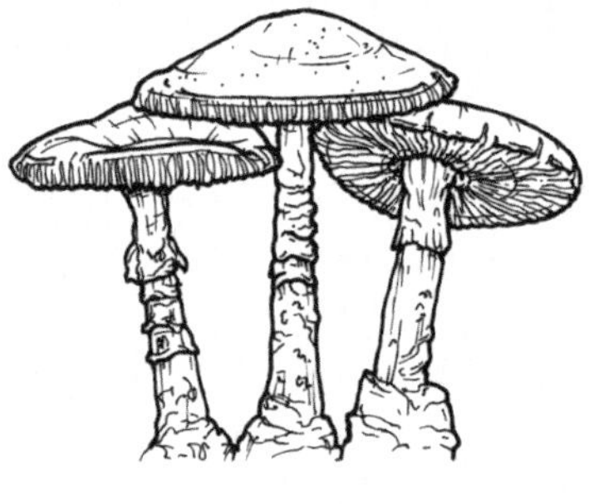
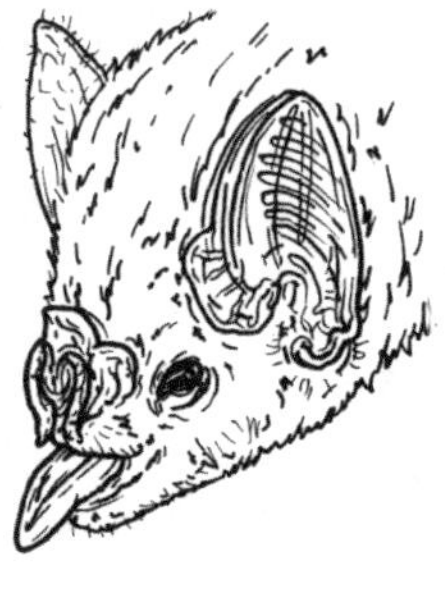
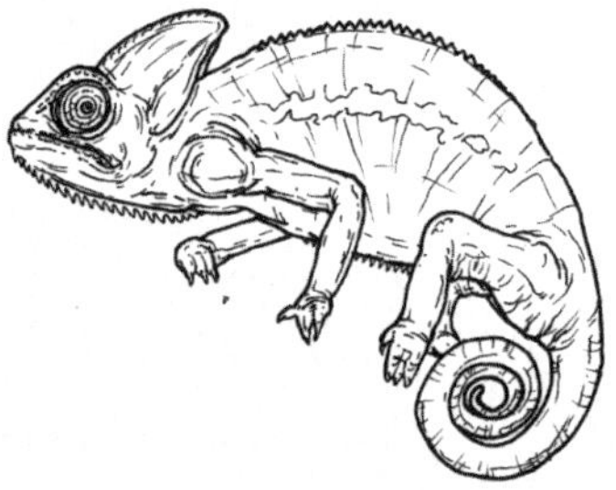
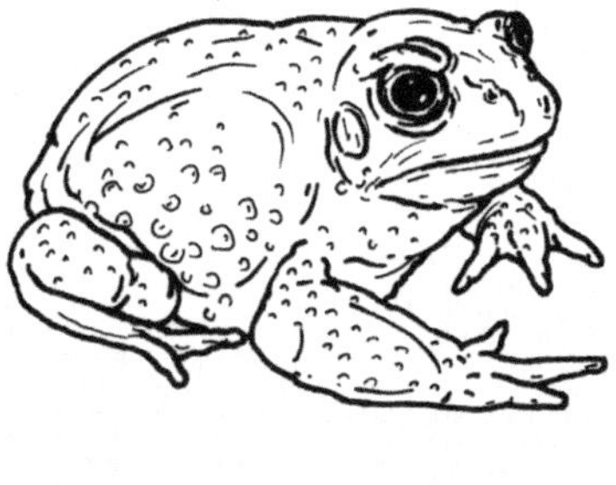
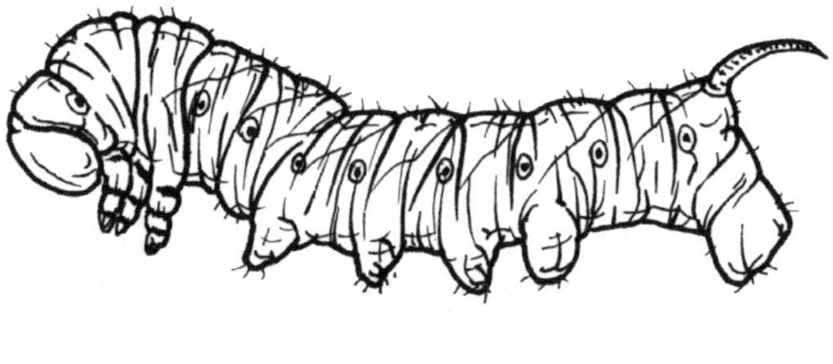